BEYOND REGULAR HABITS

The Journey Towards Success and Achieving Goals

BY
Elsie Gabe

Beyond Regular Habits

Copyright © 2024 by Elsie Gabe

All rights reserved. Except for brief quotations and certain other noncommercial uses allowed by copyright law, no part of this book may be copied, transmitted, or distributed in any form or by any means, including photocopying, recording, or other electronic methods, without the author's prior written permission.

Non-fiction is what this book, "Beyond Regular Habits: The Journey Towards Achieving Goals and Success," is. The content is only meant to be used for informative and educational purposes. However, regardless of whether errors or omissions are the result of carelessness, an accident, or any other cause, they do not assume and hereby disclaim any duty to any party for any loss, damage, or disruption caused by errors or omissions.

Elsie Gabe alone is the author and her opinions are her own. Any likeness to real people, living or dead, or to real things is entirely coincidental.

Beyond Regular Habits

ABOUT THE AUTHOR

Elsie Gabe is well known for her insightful writings on mental health, growth and habits. She offers her work a great passion for personal growth and a lot of expertise.

Over her career, Gabe has continually spoken about the need to develop habits that propel success and personal development.

In her book, "Beyond Regular Habits: The Journey Towards Achieving Goals and Success," Gabe gives practical advice built on her understanding of mental health. Her work not only offers readers actionable plans but also motivates them to cultivate good habits that brings productivity.

Apart from her creative activities, Elsie Gabe actively guides future authors and professionals, therefore developing their leadership qualities. She is still committed to ensuring people are their best in both personal and professional domains.

Beyond Regular Habits

TABLE OF CONTENTS

ABOUT THE AUTHOR
TABLE OF CONTENTS
WHAT'S YOUR STORY???
INTRODUCTION
The Cycle of Habits: Behavioral patterns
CHAPTER 1
Confronting Limiting Beliefs
CHAPTER 2
The keystone Habits Of Failure
CHAPTER 3
Understanding Resistance
CHAPTER 4
Success Redefined
CHAPTER 5
Mapping Out Goals
CHAPTER 6
Rewiring The Brain
CHAPTER 7
Fostering A Growth Mindset
CHAPTER 8
Morning Visualization
CHAPTER 9
Reflective Journaling
CHAPTER 10
Digital Detox
CHAPTER 11

Time Mastery
CHAPTER 12
Leveraging Social Support
CHAPTER 13
The Roots And Remedies
CONCLUSION
Success Stories

WHAT'S YOUR STORY???

The thought of success is sometimes like a flame. It lights up our souls and helps to move us forward on our journey through life. No matter how difficult things get, the thought of it sometimes helps us refuel. Success is not just about ticking off goals on a checklist; it's about embracing the adventures, facing the challenges head-on, and emerging victorious against all odds.

But let's be real for a moment – Is the road to success always a smooth one? No. It's always full of twists, turns, and unexpected incidents that can leave even the most determined traveler feeling lost and disheartened. From battling inner demons like self-doubt and fear of failure to wrestling with external forces that's beyond our control, it's a constant struggle.

Let me tell you about this young woman, Maya. Living in the bustling city of New York, amidst the towering skyscrapers and bustling streets, her life was one big monotonous pattern. There was nothing fun and exciting. There was no buzz, no color, absolutely nothing that would bring peace and joy.

It was just the regular trend of her work as an underpaid salesgirl, the stress that came with her part time study, the responsibility she had towards her parents, siblings and her abusive relationship. Maya had always dreamed of making a difference in the world, but like many, she found herself caught in the daily grind of life and the struggle to break free from the monotony was unending.

One evening, as Maya sat in her cramped apartment, surrounded by piles of unfinished work and unfulfilled dreams, she stumbled upon an old journal tucked away in a forgotten corner. Her curiosity was piqued and she dusted it off. Flipping through its weathered pages, she found the scribbles of her younger self, full of hope and ambition.

As she let her eyes scan through pages, she noticed they're filled with the stories of her past aspirations. The goals she once set but never pursued and the dreams that seemed out of reach. With each turn of the page, she felt tears at the corner of her eyes.

She smiled amidst the tears flowing down her cheeks as she remembered a scenario where her six-year old self was happily telling her mom how she'll become a musician and travel all over the world. Though she can't imagine herself with a mic singing before a crowd now, she definitely still yearned to be successful.

As Maya closed the journal, she felt a spark and she let a smile tug at the corners of her lips. The journal in her hands lies not just the story of her past, but a plan for her future—a future filled with unlimited potential and so many opportunities for growth and fulfillment. She suddenly wanted every single dream accomplished. The inspiration was all in her head and the resolve to rewrite her story was so strong within her.

Determined for a change in her life, Maya began to work towards self-discovery and transformation. She reset her goals boldly, started pulling down all her self-imposed limitations, and became relentlessly persistent.

Rome wasn't built in a day and of course it took a long while, but her unwavering determination began to turn her dreams into reality. One small step at a time. Even when the storms came and she experienced setbacks and challenges, Maya stood firm in her pursuit of success. She began to embrace failure as a stepping stone to growth and to celebrate every small victory, no matter how small.

And as she neared the summit of her aspirations, Maya realized that the true measure of success was not found in reaching the destination but in the journey itself.

Looking at her today, her story serves as an example of hope and inspiration. A living testament to the importance of perseverance and diligence.

Her story is a reminder to all that no dream is too big and no goal is unreachable. This is for only those who dare to believe in themselves and their ability to create their own destiny.

So, right about now, I want you to think about your own tale. Which dreams are inside you, ready to come to life? What goals beckon you to take that first courageous step? What is that ambition, goal, purpose that you so desire to achieve but seems like it's a milestone away? What's your story?

Beyond Regular Habits

INTRODUCTION

The Dynamics of Habit

The symphony of our lives is shaped by the melody of repetition and the beat of routine. Human behavior is fundamentally shaped by habit, which determines our attitudes, deeds, and eventually, our fate. It is not merely a thoughtless routine or a repetitive action. But what exactly is a habit?

At its essence, habit is the automatic response of the brain to a particular situation or cue, triggered by the repetition of a specific behavior and reinforced by a reward or consequence. These behaviors become regular with time, often without conscious thought.

It is also a routine behavior that is founded on recurrent exposure to the same kind of environmental stimuli.

Regardless of whether the intended outcome is attained, these signals cause an automatic link to form between the cue and the subsequent behavior. The basic idea is that actions that are repeated often enough become ordinary and habitual, taking them out of the conscious mind's focus.

Contextual cues give behaviors precedence over cognitive goals because they trigger the associated habit. Although habits can be acquired implicitly or consciously, both methods of assimilation are frequently used in conjunction.

Since the late 1800s, psychologists have been examining habits. The concept of habits is closely related to the stimulus-response model of classical behaviorism, as both theories believe that behavior is a reaction to external events.

Nevertheless, the majority of modern psychologists and cognitive scientists believe that habits relate to inner dispositions rather than their outward expressions, contrary to classical behaviorism's denial that inner state of mind, such as valued objectives, would have nothing significant to do with it. While classical links habits to external events, modern psychology emphasizes internal motivations. To differentiate overt conduct from internal dispositions, the latter are frequently referred to as routines.

It may seem confusing to distinguish between routines and dispositions, but considering habits as the dispositions that lead to routine behavior—or not—leaves open the possibility that habits persist even when their expression is obstructed.

Although they are still potentialities for action, they are just waiting for the ideal circumstances to materialize. Simply put, habits persist even when their expression is hindered, waiting for suitable circumstances. Philosophy has historically used the concept of habit, and more recently, the social sciences have as well.

Social scientists are more interested in how habits help make groups work. But psychologists focus more on how habits might help us understand what's going on in our minds when we're not aware of it. Social scientists and social theorists can use this method to look at both the basic social aspects of our lives and the physiological bases of action.

Sociology and anthropology both look at habits from the point of view of socialization and enculturation. This is why the idea of habit is used to show how behavior is linked to a society that most people share. A lot of the time, "popular science" talks about habits and how to stop what are called "bad habits."

Ye,the dynamics of habit are as diverse and multifaceted as the individuals who express them. What compels one person to reach for the stars while another chooses the common environment? What drives some people to embrace change with open arms while others cling desperately to the safety of familiarity?

The answers are in the web of cues, habits, and benefits that make us do what we do. These are shaped by our very own genes, surroundings, and our own experiences. Much deeper than what we see, habits have a huge effect on our lives and can be seen in a lot of different situations.

From the early riser who effortlessly embraces the dawn of each day to the chronic procrastinator who perennially postpones their dreams, habit weaves its intricate web through the fabric of our existence, dictating the patterns of our thoughts, actions, and ultimately, our destinies.

The Cycle of Habits: Behavioral patterns

Did you know that habits control over half of our waking hours? It's surprising how our brains, on their own, form patterns that function automatically once they're set.

Although useful, this efficiency is indiscriminate, storing both beneficial and harmful habits.

Certain habits are helpful to us, much like how you've learnt to drive a car with ease. On the other hand, some behaviors, like acting without thinking when you're lonely or eating when you're upset, may be bad.

It takes more than resolve to break a habit; you also need to know what triggers, routines, and rewards they provide. To initiate change, it is important to identify the triggers that trigger these behaviors. For example, a person who struggles with commitment may feel pressured to go on dates as the weekends draw near in order to avoid feeling alone. Identifying this trigger makes it possible to change the procedure.

Identifying the pattern and changing one's behavior are more important than placing the blame on oneself. These patterns which some individuals call 'The cycle of Habits' or 'The Habit Loop' is what defines it all.

- **The Habit Loop: What is it?**

The brain is always searching for effective ways to carry out tasks. When the brain cycles and retains knowledge to make tasks easier, a habit loop develops.

Beyond Regular Habits

Understanding these cycles and how some behaviors you exhibit become problems in your life is important.

- **How Does the Habit Loop Get Defined?**

Frequent repetition of the same activities drills information about our responses into the brain. The habit loop looks like this. Habit loops are a basic aspect of our daily functioning.

Habits are efficient processes, for instance, because they enable people to complete routine tasks—like brewing coffee in the morning—without giving them any attention. Your energy is stored for things that require systematic reasoning.

The brain does not distinguish between the different kinds of knowledge it stores, though. It reads emotions and bodily reactions for cues. When people respond in the same way to specific stimuli, the brain introduces stress reactions.

Anxiety loops are produced by this. Therefore, even in non-serious situations, the brain receives signals from the body and initiates all system defenses. People develop anxiety habit loops when they repeatedly overreact to stress. Even if they might not be useful reactions to the current situation, the brain will connect to the same loops after it has been trained to react in a particular way.

- **Understanding the Habit Loop**

The cycle of Cue, Routine, and Reward is a basic yet central idea at the core of the habit loop. It starts with a cue, an environmental trigger that causes us to act in a particular way.

This could be anything at all, such as an inward sensation or emotion or a well-known sight, sound, or scent. We move into the routine phase after detecting the cue, during which we carry out the cue-associated habitual activity.

This practice usually requires minimal conscious thinking or effort because it is instinctive and ingrained. We finally arrive at the reward phase, where we get the desired results or emotions that motivate us to carry out the activity again in the future and strengthen the habit.

The anatomy of behavior goes into detail on how each component of the habit loop shapes our behavior and decision-making process. The small things that set off our habits, the automatic things we do, and the rewards that make us want to do them again are all important parts of the habit loop that determines how we act and what happens to us.

- **How Do Loops of Habits Form?**

Habit loops evolved over time to help people manage the vast volumes of data that are constantly being input into our brains. The brain can react to a range of inputs reliably thanks to these feedback loops.

This is how an effective, self-regulating system gets identified. Nevertheless, the best possible classification is done by any system processing large amounts of data, though this does not always result in the best results. Researchers have connected the acquisition of habits to the forebrain's basal ganglia. This is the point at which habit cycles and automatic learning occur. Here are three components of a habit cycle along with several instances of habit loops:

1. CUE
A habit is set off by a cue. Cues are strong reactions to environmental factors that come from outside sources. For instance, you would quickly pull your automobile over to the side of the road if you heard an emergency siren while driving.

Your brain is programmed to react automatically to the auditory stimulus. When you hear it, no matter where you are, you start to react to it automatically. Your brain is therefore programmed to obey cues, and you derive satisfaction from acting morally.

2. ROUTINE
The habit is the routine. This is the behavioral cycle that is brought on by different triggers. If food trucks are cooking outside your place of business, this may serve as a daily reminder that lunch is approaching. Maybe all you do is stop over for a quick snack.

There are numerous unfavorable causes for anxious behavior loops. For example, walking past a coffee shop can become an uncomfortable trigger if you met someone for coffee and had a bad experience. Triggers for anxiety might be everywhere, and some start to completely shun awkward situations.

3. REWARD
Your desire for specific results is what drives you to repeat acts in order to get the reward. When a situation resembles this one in the future, the brain's neural connections are prone to recall this information thanks to positive reinforcement.

Unwanted behaviors may also fall under this feedback loop. When an anxious person practices avoidance or makes plans to keep oneself safe, they feel relieved. The brain receives and stores these signals even though the behaviors are unhealthy. Emotional escape is the prize.

It's important to always recall that habit cycles would help people establish simple daily routines that relieves stress and tiredness. As you keep doing this, you can increase your level of productivity and save energy. However, habit cycles become harmful to wellbeing when stress and worry cause bodily and emotional reactions to become out of synchrony.

Beyond Regular Habits

THE STRUGGLES

Strength and growth comes only through continuous effort and struggle ~ Napoleon Hill

Beyond Regular Habits

CHAPTER 1

Confronting Limiting Beliefs

Let's go back to our childhood. Consider your earliest childhood recollections. They must be memories of your fearlessness, embracing the unknown without anxiety or tension. You simply completed the task. You either grabbed a lizard or dove into the water, however I would strongly suggest avoiding the elderly reptiles. You understand what I mean.

It is advantageous that the area of the brain responsible for causing anxiety was still developing. We are so incredibly delighted that, as kids, we are living our best lives here on Earth. We are completely worry-free! As we get older, the rules come from the environment around us. What you should and shouldn't do is prescribed to you. There are some things we shouldn't say—you know, it's not very "ladylike"—and some ways we should dress, especially as women.

I won't go into too much detail about patriarchy because it's a topic for another time, but these rules you live by probably have ingrained limiting ideas and mental barriers that are preventing you from maximizing your full potential. The biggest barriers we face on the path to personal development are frequently mental ones. Limiting ideas that have been engrained through years of experience and conditioning might undermine our attempts to form virtuous habits and accomplish our objectives.

What are limiting beliefs and mental blocks?
Negative thought patterns such as mental barriers and limiting beliefs might hinder us from reaching our objectives. They can result in cognitive distortions including overgeneralization, catastrophizing, and leaping to conclusions. They are typically based in self-doubt.

These mental roadblocks have the potential to overwhelm us with worry and terror, leaving us with hopelessness and powerlessness. We can start challenging these mental obstacles and limiting ideas by challenging the veracity of our beliefs once we become aware of them. Personal development can be seriously hampered by mental obstacles and restrictive beliefs. To get past these mental obstacles and restricting ideas, it's critical to pinpoint their underlying origins.

Whether you're experiencing poor self-esteem, feeling trapped in your profession, or any other type of personal growth obstacle, it's critical to stand back and examine the underlying causes of your mental obstacles. We are able to remove the obstacles that prevent us from leading the greatest lives possible thanks to this approach. We can begin the process of developing a more positive mindset that will support us in achieving our objectives by becoming aware of our own negative thought patterns. The process involves;

I. Determine Which Beliefs Are Self-Limiting
The initial phase of this life-changing adventure is identifying the self-limiting ideas that prevent you from moving forward. These are frequently unconsciously held ideas or opinions that put artificial restrictions on your potential. They may have to do with your knowledge, aptitude, or talents, and it's critical to recognize them since they can impede your development.

How do you do this?

- Self-Reflection: I make time for introspection and self-examination. I thought back to instances where fear or self-doubt had caused me to withdraw.
- Journaling: I found that writing down my thoughts and feelings, particularly when I was doubting my skills or ability, was helpful.
- Requesting Input: I made an effort to get input from mentors, family members, and friends. Frequently, their insights made self-limiting ideas that I was partially unaware of clear.
- Professional Help: I occasionally went to a therapist or counselor who specialized in treating deeply ingrained self-limiting beliefs for assistance. Their advice was really helpful in identifying and addressing these constraints.

II. Recast Your Ideas

It's time to confront and reframe these self-limiting ideas after you've discovered them. The intention is to change these negative ideas into empowering affirmations that will increase your self-esteem and enable you to take use of your advantages.

The process includes;
- Awareness: I tried hard to recognize these self-limiting ideas as soon as they came up. It

was important to be mindful of one's negative self-talk.
- Examine Your ideas: I kept asking myself if these restrictive ideas were really true. I questioned whether I could find any proof to back them up or refute them.
- Replace with Affirmations: I made affirmations that were positive and addressed these negative ideas. I changed phrases like "I can't do this" to something like "I am capable and up to the task"
- Visualization: This was a significant factor. To bolster my newly discovered positive attitudes, I used visualization to picture myself succeeding and reaching my objectives.
- Practice Mindfulness: I was able to observe and disengage from negative thoughts by practicing mindfulness and meditation.
- Consistency: Repeating affirmations and encouraging self-talk on a regular basis was necessary to rewire mental processes.
- Seek Support: Encouraging friends or a coach along the way provided an additional level of accountability and support.

III. Have a Positive Support System Around You

Creating a supportive network is essential to overcoming self-limiting ideas. It's like having a strong wind behind you when you surround yourself with individuals who support and believe in your aspirations. They can provide insightful advice, accountability, and direction.

How do you accomplish this?
- Assess present Relationships: I examined my present social circle more closely and noted those people who encouraged and supported me on a regular basis.
- Seek Like-Minded Communities: Finding a supportive environment was made easy by joining clubs or communities that shared my interests.
- Express Your Aspirations: It felt liberating to talk honestly about my aspirations and ambitions with my network of support. A sense of accountability was formed when I confided in mentors or close friends about my struggles and achievements.
- Seek Advice: I didn't think twice to ask my support system for help or direction when I needed it. They gave me new thoughts and a different viewpoint.
- Minimize Negative Influences: I noted the connections that regularly encouraged skepticism or negativity. It was crucial for me to limit my exposure to these influences in order to keep a good outlook.

IV. Act Now and Confront Your Fears

Facing our darkest fears is often necessary in order to confront self-limiting ideas. I've come to the conclusion that it's critical to recognize that fear is a normal component of this process.

Feeling it is normal; the important thing is to avoid letting it stop you. Leaving your comfort zone with tiny, calculated moves is the first step toward overcoming your concerns.

You can do the following;
- Divide Work into Smaller Steps: I divided my objectives into more doable, smaller jobs. This lets me see a clear route to achievement in addition to making them seem less intimidating.
- Accept Uncomfort: I realized that experiencing discomfort is a sign of progress. Rather than running from it, I discovered how to welcome it as a sign of growth and development.
- Establish a Timeline: Giving each task a deadline helped to provide structure and accountability. It's incredible how using a timeline can increase your drive.
- Seek Accountability: I told a mentor or close friend about my action plan. Their encouragement and accountability for my advancement were both provided via their support.

- Visualize Success: I found that staying motivated and boosting my confidence came from spending time envisioning the successful result of my activities. One effective technique to help you stay focused on your objectives is visualization.

The following variables affect self-limiting beliefs:

Your limiting beliefs and mental blockages have been shaped by a variety of life experiences. Here are a handful that you may find relatable.

- **Family**

It's possible that as a child, your parents and relatives imposed their values and ideas on you. That might have been impacted by their own childhood as well as by parental practices, religion, and culture. They might have desired for you to have a particular outlook on life, exhibit particular behaviors, or perhaps they predetermined your job path for you when you were very little.

For instance, you could develop the limiting notion that you are unworthy if your parents are judgmental and always point out little mistakes or inconsistencies in everything you do, even if they are not malicious. You consequently put off taking advantage of opportunities or put things off because you believe they won't be worthwhile and will lead to failure.

- **Friends**

You become the people you associate with. It's been stated that the five individuals you spend the most time with determine who you are on average. Our friends can have a significant impact on our life and help mold our morals and ideas.

It's critical to surround ourselves with positive role models, but it's also critical to recognize the potential negative effects of our friends' limiting ideas. We must be careful not to let those with pessimistic attitudes about life affect us, as this could result in the development of restrictive beliefs that could keep us from reaching our objectives.

- **Experiences**

Everybody has had periods in their lives when they were afraid, hesitant, or doubtful. These encounters may cause us to form restrictive ideas that prevent us from reaching our objectives. By identifying these misconceptions and taking action to dispel them, we can give ourselves access to a world of opportunities. By comprehending how our experiences have influenced our beliefs, we may begin to dismantle the obstacles preventing us from thinking and acting in ways that make more sense to us.

You can start taking concrete measures to overcome your mental obstacles by identifying the underlying problems that are producing them. This will assist you in continuing on your path to achievement and personal development.

The Impact of Goals and Habits on Mental Health

Our ability to pursue and accomplish our goals, as well as how our habits are formed, are greatly influenced by our mental health. Maintaining consistency in our behavior and staying focused on our goals becomes more difficult when our mental health is affected.

Our confidence and motivation can be undermined by negative thought patterns and self-limiting beliefs, which can result in procrastination, self-doubt, and failure-related fear. These mental obstacles produce a vicious loop that hinders our development and feeds into our self-defeating ideas about our capacities.

Additionally, stress, anxiety, and depression can disturb our cognitive functioning and impair our decision-making skills, making it harder to set realistic objectives, prioritize activities, and stay resilient in the face of adversity. Our attempts to develop successful habits and overcome these underlying mental health difficulties are likely to be hindered.

Overcoming Limiting Beliefs and Mental Blocks

Isn't it amazing how much this situation depends on our perceptions? How diverse people's memories of a single instant in time can be. How might a single moment in time have the potential to change someone's life while having no bearing on another?

Consider the scenario where you were playing fetch with your sister at a family get-together and all of a sudden you stumbled and fell in front of the family. Your play-fighting sibling may recall this as a little rough and tumble when you were younger, or they may not recall it at all. However, you personally connect this memory with feelings of fear, shame, or sadness.

I want you to consider eight life-defining events. These are the times that you can still clearly remember and are associated with powerful feelings. They can be either positive or negative, but they are typically negative when it comes to mental obstacles and limiting beliefs.

Put these in writing. This will provide you more insight into how your current identity came to be and help you understand yourself a little better.

Techniques for Getting Past Mental Obstacles

1. Determine and Face Limiting thoughts

Recognizing and facing the unfavorable thoughts that are preventing us from moving forward is the first step in breaking through mental obstacles. Through challenging the veracity of these ideas and reinterpreting them in a more constructive context, we can initiate a mental transformation and foster an increased sense of self-assurance and capability.

2. Practice Self-Compassion

To overcome mental obstacles and develop resilience in the face of adversity requires the cultivation of self-compassion. We may increase our sense of self-worth and acceptability by being kind and understanding to ourselves. This will enable us to overcome our obstacles and follow our objectives with courage and tenacity.

3. Develop a Growth Mindset

Rather than seeing problems as insurmountable hurdles, adopting a growth mindset means seeing challenges as chances for personal development and education. We can develop a stronger feeling of resilience and optimism in the pursuit of our goals by reinterpreting setbacks as worthwhile learning opportunities and enjoying the process of self-improvement.

4. Practice Mindfulness and Stress Management
Mindfulness techniques, such as yoga, meditation, and deep breathing exercises, can help reduce stress and anxiety, which enhances our capacity for perspective, concentration, and decision-making. We may increase our mental clarity and emotional resilience by implementing these techniques into our daily lives. This will make it easier for us to overcome mental obstacles and accomplish our objectives.

5. Seek Support and Accountability
We can overcome mental obstacles and stay on track to achieve our objectives far more easily when we are surrounded by people who hold us accountable for our actions and who believe in our potential. Seeking out support and encouragement from others—whether from friends, family, mentors, or professional coaches—can offer priceless inspiration and direction on our path to success.

How to Cultivate a positive Outlook

Although there are things in your life beyond your control, you can manage your thoughts. Your perspective on the world determines your reaction to it. You'll be more inclined to derive significance from each and every one of your encounters if you think that everything occurs for a reason. If you think everyone is against you, then every setback will seem like a personal assault on your dignity.

Thinking positively isn't limited to when things are going well for someone; it also refers to how we handle obstacles and disappointments. We are more likely to overcome obstacles with less stress and worry if we regard them as chances for personal development and advancement rather than as dangers to our happiness or identity.

These three approaches will help you cultivate a happy outlook;

1. Show appreciation for what you have. Gratitude is the first step toward changing your mindset. Embracing gratitude is a potent technique that can help you change your viewpoint and have a happier outlook on life. It's also a fantastic method to get back in touch with who you are, which will make you feel more centered and in control.

Either in a gratitude journal or on your phone (you may use an app like Gratitude Journal), list three things for which you are thankful every day. This makes it easier to monitor how frequently you perform this exercise and how long it has been since you last performed it.

2. Engage in a daily activity that improves your mental health and makes you feel good about yourself, even if it's as easy as taking a bath or brushing your teeth. You must give your mind the same daily care as your body. You're more likely to be able to handle life's obstacles if you take better care of it and maintain its condition.

3. Prioritize your controllable aspects over your uncontrollable ones. Although you have no influence over what other people think of you, you do have power over how you respond to them. While it's not always possible to achieve your goals, if you concentrate on the good things that are already happening in your life, you'll find it easier to be thankful for the opportunities that do present themselves.

It is entirely beyond your ability to predict when or where a tragedy will occur, so why waste time worrying about it? It's critical that you take action to develop and sustain a positive mindset if you want to stay cheerful and psychologically well.

To achieve this, try writing down three positive things that happened every day for a week (or longer), practicing gratitude, constantly reminding yourself of your objectives and the reasons behind them.

Also, keep your attention on the things that you can control rather than the things that are out of your control, even when it seems like nothing positive is happening at the moment.

CHAPTER 2

The keystone Habits Of Failure

In general, people have misconceptions about failure.

Was that afternoon a failure if you go out to shoot a video, return with a ton of footage, and then find it's all wrong? Was it a failure if you spent an hour brainstorming ideas for a project with your team and came away with nothing but additional questions? Was the first draft a failure if, after writing the entire book, you suddenly realize in the conclusion what it was you were truly trying to communicate?

It isn't real at all. If you gain any worthwhile knowledge from it, it is not a failure. Accordingly, the following nine well-known personas represent those who "fail" frequently as well as the things you should try your hardest to avoid:

1. They Focus On The Bad Rather Than The Good
If you're too busy criticizing yourself, how are you going to learn? The correlating mindset makes the difference between someone who stumbles and learns from it and someone who stumbles and whines about it. They both fell nonetheless. How they each chose to see that particular situation makes a difference.

2. They Have Impractical Expectations
Yes, you will probably fail if your side business brings in zero dollars annually and you aim to make seven figures in the upcoming year. It's not reasonable to anticipate that. It's also impractical, so you'll be viewed as a failure no matter where you end up.

3. They Never Seek Assistance
I wish you luck in assuming you can handle everything by yourself. Individuals who don't succeed prepare themselves for failure by a long shot. Even though they are aware of their needs, they won't acknowledge them. That does not increase your strength or drive. You are therefore not intelligent. Request assistance.

4. They Speak More Often Than Act

It is not the same to talk about something and not act upon it. An idea does not guarantee that it will be carried out, or carried out well. People fail because they are blind to the shortcomings in their routines. One bad habit that many "wantrapreneurs" have in common is that they love to talk about what they're going to do but find it difficult to put their plans into action.

5. They Are Afraid to Share Their Ideas
Nobody is going to pilfer your business concept. Really? It is more naïve than respectable to believe that the concept you came up with this morning in the shower is something that should be kept secret from the public. Mind-blowing ideas are extremely rare. You can't just go around bragging to people, "I have this great idea, but I can't tell them yet." You can't really proceed with it after that.

6. They Won't Give Up Ownership
I have strong feelings about project ownership because I don't think money alone can inspire the best work. Equitable ownership is not limited to "on paper" ownership. It also involves having an emotional connection. Additionally, team members who share your level of emotional investment will perform at their highest level.

Individuals that struggle to create productive teams and products frequently attempt to retain an excessive amount of ownership for themselves, and even worse, they become irate when others don't share their enthusiasm for the concept.

Would you like to work with people that are somewhat emotionally invested in the company, yet retain more equity for yourself? Or divide that equity and require complete emotional investment from every member of your team? The response is obvious.

7. They Assemble Around People Who See Failure As An Option

If everyone around you seems OK with failing, how in the world are you going to succeed? It is not possible. According to the proverb, "Misery loves company." Those that have a good outlook on life associate with other positive thinkers.

8. They Follow What Is Popular Instead Of What Is Right

Though it can take many different forms, hubris is a common way for failure to manifest. You don't always need to do something just because you can. Individuals become arrogant, overconfident, and attempt to fit in with the trend rather than using their unique set of skills.

9. They Consider giving up as a possibility

People who don't even consider failure as an option are the ones who actually succeed and accomplish their goals in life. Once more, it's a mindset-based idea. What you make of failure is up to you. You give it your own definition. Furthermore, the more power you grant it, the more you define it.

Exposing The Fundamental Failure Habits

It's critical to comprehend the routines that impede us as well as the personalities of those that ultimately fail. These are deeply rooted behavioral patterns that serve as roadblocks in our way of achievement.

They work quietly in the background, affecting our decisions, attitudes, and behaviors in subtle ways. The ingrained patterns of failure—the subliminal behaviors that impede our advancement and limit our potential—are exposed below.

- **Procrastination:** Postponing activities or choices, frequently due to anxiety or uncertainty, results in lost chances and unrealized potential. Perfectionism, fear of failing, and low self-esteem are all possible causes of procrastination. It's the practice of putting off crucial activities till the very last minute, which leads to needless stress and subpar outcomes.

- **Self-sabotage**: Taking part in actions, such self-doubt, self-criticism, failure-apprehension and all others that undercut our own achievement.

Self-sabotage can take many different forms, from participating in self-destructive actions that impede our progress to coming up with justifications for not pursuing our goals. It is the tendency to stand in our own way and undermine our own efforts before they ever have a chance to be successful.

- **Negative self-talk:** This is the habit of having a negative or gloomy internal discourse that lowers resilience and undermines self-worth.

There are numerous different ways that negative self-talk manifests itself, ranging from severe self-criticism to doomsday scenarios. It's the tendency to continuously berate ourselves, have self-doubt, and assume the worst in all circumstances.

- **Perfectionism:** Having extremely high expectations and becoming upset or avoiding situations when they can't be met, which leaves one paralyzed or unable to make progress.

  Fear of rejection or failure is a common source of perfectionism, which pushes us to perform flawlessly in order to feel validated. It's the tendency to avoid making mistakes, aim for unreachable goals, and never feel content with our work.

- **Absence of goal-setting:** Aimless pacing and directionlessness might result from a failure to establish specific, attainable goals. It's simple to get overwhelmed or lose motivation when there aren't any clear goals to strive for.

- **Negative comparison:** Continually comparing oneself to others—especially negatively—can lead to low self-esteem and feelings of inadequacy. This behavior can undermine one's sense of worth and take attention away from one's own development.

- **Fear of failure:** Letting fear of failure control one's behavior can lead to avoidance of risks or difficulties, which eventually reduces one's chances for success and personal development. This dread has the power to paralyze judgment and keep people from going for their goals.

- **Absence of self-control:** Giving in to the need for instant gratification or indulging in unimportant activities instead of setting priorities can sabotage efforts and prevent success. It is challenging to remain motivated and concentrated while working toward long-term goals when one lacks self-discipline.

- **Resistance to change:** Staying in one's comfort zone and opposing change might impede one's ability to grow both personally and professionally. This behavior eventually stops people from moving forward by preventing them from seizing new opportunities and changing with the times.

- **Time management errors:** Time management errors can cause disarray, missed deadlines, and increased stress. This behavior may leave one feeling overburdened and unable to move forward with goals in a significant way.

- **Victim mentality:** Taking on a victim mentality, in which one places the responsibility for their failures on other people or outside events, can lead to a helplessness and resignation. This kind of thinking undercuts individual autonomy and impedes proactive attempts to succeed.

- **Seeking approval from others:** Feelings of dependency and inadequacy can result from relying too much on approval from others for one's value and self-worth. This behavior undermines self-reliance and autonomy, making it more difficult to pursue objectives with commitment.

It is essential to comprehend these failure-prone habits in order to identify their influence on our life and take action to break them. By knowing all these things, it would be easier to call ourselves to order when we realize we're heading down that path. It would become remarkably easy as well to overcome self-limiting habits and patterns.

Beyond Regular Habits

CHAPTER 3

Understanding Resistance

Self-control. Determination. Willpower. Motivation

These four essential characteristics create the basis of our goals and aspirations, motivate our corresponding behaviors, and elevate our performance.

Every single person, on average, contains all four of these attributes, albeit to varying degrees of proficiency. However, these abilities are at a typical, ordinary level that arises from maturing and meeting expectations and daily obligations such as getting up, going to work or school, finishing homework, adhering to personal hygiene regulations, and making an effort to build and preserve connections.

However, We have all come across persons who exude these traits extraordinarily well; these are folks we consider to be charming, influential, and enlightened. These people are actually those of us who have figured out a particular route and approach to strengthen these four essential pillars of human performance that possess the ability to shape how others perceive them.

One of the most frequent challenges we face when trying to reach our objectives and develop healthy habits is resistance. It can take many different forms, such as self-doubt, procrastination, and temptations and diversions. This chapter will examine these four essential ideas: Motivation, Willpower, Determination and Self-Control. These ideas are critical to conquering resistance.

Let's examine the beginning and the steps that guide us down the route to achieving personal power. In the paragraphs that follow, the term "brain" refers to the actual brain, while "mind" refers to the brain's intangible component.

1. The foundation for developing personal mental toughness is discipline or you can say self-control This is the brain's initial step. It is based on suffering,

perseverance, and repeatedly performing painful and emotionally taxing tasks.

2. Willpower is the mental capacity that is derived from the consistent, observable, quantitative, and palpable strength of discipline. It provides the tenacity and concentration needed to perform consistently in the face of mental obstacles like resistance, unstable emotions, grief, loss, etc. It also holds true for achievements and avoiding becoming "spoiled" by them.

3. The mind, propelled by the erratic power of resolve, is determination. It makes it possible to focus the attention on the necessary results even when one is sidetracked by both good and bad feelings, situations, and individuals.

4. Motivation is the last stage of mental work and results; it allows focused, determined resilience for a certain set of mental goals. It's not inherently good or evil. The determination of a necessary consequence is solely a product of Peak Performance behavior on the part of the individual.

Let's now examine these ideas in greater detail.

- **Self-Control**

The capacity to control one's ideas, feelings, and actions in order to achieve long-term objectives is known as self-control. It entails making deliberate decisions that support our interests and ideals despite discomfort or temptation. Self-control is frequently linked to tenacity, consistency, and postponing gratification.

The greatest challenge with self-discipline is being consistent over an extended period of time. Maintaining a habit or action plan needs commitment and persistence, especially in the face of setbacks or waning inspiration. Furthermore, it might be difficult to establish self-control, particularly for people who are used to impulsive behavior or rapid pleasure.

Despite these difficulties, having self-control is a good quality that can help you succeed and feel more fulfilled in life. People who practice self-discipline are able to overcome obstacles and maintain focus on their objectives in the face of difficulty.

- **Willpower**

This is the capacity to withstand short-term temptations in favor of long-term objectives. It is also sometimes referred to as self-control or resolve. It entails making conscious decisions that are consistent with our goals and ideals by pushing past our impulsive or immediate desires. The ability to overcome adversity and stay on course to accomplish our goals depends on our willpower.

Willpower is a difficult concept for individuals to grasp because of its limitations. Studies have indicated that willpower is a limited resource that can be exhausted over time, particularly in situations involving stress or decision fatigue. This depletion may result in a loss of self-control and a greater openness to temptation.

Willpower has its limitations, but it may be improved with effort and awareness. People can improve their capacity to withstand temptation and maintain discipline in the face of their objectives by becoming aware of their triggers and putting tactics to conserve willpower into practice, such as creating routines and making fewer decisions.

- **Motivation**

Our activities and behaviors are propelled by motivation. It includes the will, vigor, and excitement to work for our objectives and get over challenges. Extrinsic motivation is influenced by incentives or rewards from outside sources, but intrinsic motivation comes from inside.

Long-term momentum maintenance is one of the biggest challenges people have while trying to stay motivated. Numerous variables, including mood, surroundings, and outside events, might affect motivation. People who lack motivation may feel doubtful, put off achieving their goals, or become uninterested in doing so.

Despite these obstacles, motivation can be fostered and maintained in a number of ways, including by establishing specific objectives. Also, picturing accomplishment, and enlisting the help of others. People can overcome opposition and maintain motivation in the pursuit of their goals by connecting their activities with their values and passions and by drawing on their innate motivations.

- **Determination**

Driven by passion and resiliency, determination is a steadfast commitment to overcome challenges and achieve goals. It goes beyond simply being willing to pursue goals.

In contrast to motivation, which is subject to change based on outside factors, determination is an innate trait that perseveres through hardship. It represents the idea that all is achievable if one is persistent, hardworking, and persistent.

Resilience is one of the traits that characterizes determination. Determined people don't give up in the face of difficulties or setbacks; instead, they see them as chances for development and education. They recover from setbacks with increased vigor, utilizing them as motivation to move closer to their objectives.

Grit is another important component of determination. According to a renowned psychologist, grit is "perseverance and passion for long-term goals." Gritty people are able to maintain focus on their goals even in the face of adversity because they have a strong sense of enthusiasm and persistence. They know exactly what they want to do and are prepared to put in the time, energy, and effort required to get there.

Furthermore, tenacity is contagious. Others are motivated to work harder and pursue their own objectives when they see the steadfast dedication and resiliency of strong people. Others are inspired to believe in themselves and follow their dreams with fervor and purpose when someone possesses determination.

Similarities And Differences

Although self-control, determination, motivation, and willpower are related ideas, their underlying principles and practical uses are different. Establishing dependable routines and habits is a key component of self-discipline in order to sustain long-term goal progress.

The capacity to withstand transient temptations and maintain concentration on our goals in the face of setbacks or diversions is known as willpower. Our activities are propelled by motivation, which also fuels our desire to overcome obstacles and seek our objectives.

Characterized by resilience and tenacity, determination is the unwavering resolve and devotion to accomplishing one's goals. These ideas, however different, have one thing in common: they want us to overcome obstacles and stick with our goals.

For the sake of your achievements, they work best together: self-control gives us the structure for taking consistent action; willpower helps us avoid distractions and temptations; motivation drives our zeal and determination; and determination keeps us moving forward in the face of difficulty.

These attributes are probably the ones that make parents, bosses, and trainers shake their heads and wonder where the good individuals from their youth have disappeared, perhaps in all spheres of industry, education, and life. Parents lament the passing and attribute it to a lack of values and the modern conveniences of life.

Building Capacity

Let's get into the specific process of developing these four attributes. I would suggest that suffering and adversity are the only ways to develop tough life and discipline, which is the first stage.

Pain and suffering are well-documented manifestations of brain physiology, and legendary figures such as Mother Teresa, Abraham Lincoln, Benjamin Franklin, Gandhi, and Rockefeller are examples of discipline via hard life. Individuals who, in spite of the unpleasant pressures around them, inspire and pursue their own goals.

This is another reason why painful exercise is excellent for strengthening the force of discipline. Pressing through a weightlifting session produces an intense burn. Hard jogging with weights in your bare feet—you have to feel it to believe it. Martial arts that punch, kick, stretch, and reach beyond human limitations.

Martial arts and certain dance styles are suitable for beginning students as young as three. It is the pinnacle of physical power that enhances mental capacity, which directly translates into superior thinking ability. Discipline makes willpower an automatic byproduct of consistent effort. The association is linear, extending from the lowest points of poor performance—when you overindulge in alcohol or sweets and turn acidic when you should be dry and alkaline—to the highest points of good performance.

Finding a purpose that you know is difficult to fulfill but has been an unfulfilled dream for the better portion of your life is all it takes to manifest willpower. It is an actual component of your internal drive. The next piece that fits into place when you start using your willpower in the actual world to accomplish something observable and potentially significant is determination.

Giving up procrastination is an obvious example of resolve fueled by discipline and willpower. Working with your peers to get success and the necessary results at work, or with your family to raise its performance level, is equally important. Only when the other three keys—discipline, willpower, and determination—are in play will the last key—motivation—appear.

An innate "need" (as opposed to a "want") that is starting to firmly establish itself in the real world is what drives motivation. Because the other three required keys to unlock, power, and sustain the motivation have not been present, it has not been able to materialize up to this point. Your inner dreams are now prepared to break free from the limitations of your previously weak body, brain, and mind since all four keys are in place.

Ask yourself before moving on.

What and who am I?

Beyond Regular Habits

THE PROCESS

Searching and learning is where the miracle process all begins ~ Jim Rohn

CHAPTER 4

Success Redefined

"Success" is one of the most emotionally laden terms there is. And a portion of this can be attributed to the way that success is currently defined, which emphasizes reaching objectives and obtaining money or upward social mobility. Although many people who are technically successful yet feel that something is missing, the inference is that anything less is a failure. It could be a good idea to reconsider what success means to you or, at the very least, how you define it.

What Does Success Actually Mean? If you look into the definitions of success throughout history, you'll find that earlier meanings were equivalent to result, whether that result was favorable or unfavorable.

Two terms stand out when searching for the modern definition of success, though: accomplishment and attainment. This demonstrates how culture may have a significant impact on our viewpoints in many ways since we absorb the messages we are given about what success looks like from the people around us.

Why is this relevant? Because our viewpoints influence how we feel about not only our own acts and behaviors but also those of others. Furthermore, these often subconscious judgments have an impact on our sense of fulfillment.

The Influence of Culture on What Success Means
Because we are social animals and depend on it for existence, culture in general, and popular culture in particular, determines which acts are important enough to merit attention, something we all yearn for in one way or another. We need other people to recognize and accept who we are.

We give special attention to the accomplishments of musicians or athletes who are celebrities in many Western societies that value individual success. However, we frequently fail to recognize the contributions made by the scientists and researchers who collaborate to create life-saving medical treatments or the public officials who maintain the smooth operation of society.

These are all successful people, of course, but our attention is drawn to different things and people depending on our cultural norms and the medium that we use to communicate, including social media, news, television, and so on. The important thing to remember is that as cultures change, so does our concept of success. In a similar vein, our own definitions of success could change over time.

According to popular belief, when we are young, the people in our world are our family, friends, and community, and as we become older, our definition of success changes. But social media has changed our perception of the world and what it means to succeed in life. It can appear as though everyone is "successful"—as long as they use strict filters and only share the happiest stories—except for you.

It should therefore come as no surprise that researchers discovered a connection between social media use and depressive symptoms. The good news is that we may redefine success to suit our own needs, which is very achievable. And I wholeheartedly endorse it, particularly if you're feeling dissatisfied and concerned that you've essentially chosen success over happiness.

How to Interpret Success in a Different Way

The traditional definition of success revolves around external markers of achievement: climbing the corporate ladder, accumulating wealth, and attaining societal status. This paradigm encourages a relentless pursuit of goals driven by the desire for validation and approval from others. But when we pursue after these outward success markers, we frequently discover that we are unhappy and estranged from our actual values and passions.

It is not uncommon to see people who have attained a traditional definition of success—whether via labor or the acquisition of material possessions. However, the fact that they don't "feel" like successful people frustrates them.

Put differently, people sense a disconnection from their ideal of success. When you encounter these kinds of individuals, you would find yourself beginning to talk about the cultural forces that surround you and coming up with ways to detach yourself from them. You might then examine the distinct intersectional lens that has developed and how it fits with the conventional concept of success.

However, I think it's best to take things step by step rather than everything at once. In a coaching session, for example, we might spend time distinguishing real achievement from the "symbols of success". These symbols could include; Costly assets that depreciate (cars, boats, etc.), a house in a very desirable neighborhood, enrollment in prestigious institutions (private schools or upscale country clubs), designer apparel that, in six months, will be out of style, etc.

These success symbols just indicate a person's capacity for debt and/or propensity to spend money, occasionally both. Unfortunately, no one wins in this competition since, even though purchasing such items may bring you some happiness, there will always be someone else who is eager to spend more money.

To be clear, I'm not saying that success symbols have no place. I'm trying to convey that we need to connect with what these symbols mean to us and develop a conscious grasp of their significance. I observe a spectrum of feelings and connections with these symbols when I ask customers what meaning they have, ranging from:

"These things dictate every choice I make in life," "I deserve it because I earned it," or "This is what everyone else is doing,"

While material wealth and status may provide temporary satisfaction, they often fall short of providing lasting fulfillment and meaning. The pursuit of success at any cost can lead to burnout, stress, and a sense of emptiness. Moreover, it perpetuates a culture of comparison and competition, where individuals measure their worth based on arbitrary standards set by society.

The Need for Redefining Success

We next apply a cultural lens, and I encourage them to reflect on the ways in which they have encountered this achievement symbol in their life. Usually, there is a cultural connection since the thing or event in some way represents "success."

When I inquire about if they still feel this way about their present set of values, some will say "yes," while others will say "no." The distinction, though, is that those who answer "yes" now understand what that symbol actually means. Saying "no" also allows one to break free from the burden of guilt or the need to "keep up."

I have also dealt with people whose cultural norms give family and community great weight. However, they gave up on these ideals in order to live what they thought would be a "better" life. Many people find that the stress that follows can be too much to handle, making them rethink what success means to them.

As I've said before, success in today's fast-paced and hyper-connected world, often conjures images of wealth, status, and power. From a young age, most of us are taught to equate success with material possessions, prestigious careers, and social recognition. But as we go through life's challenges and think about our own goals, it's clear that this narrow meaning of success doesn't cover the whole range of human experience. Because of these problems, we need to quickly change the definition of success to include a bigger and more complete picture of how people can thrive.

Success shouldn't just mean accomplishments on the outside; it should also mean happiness, satisfaction, and service to others.This new meaning of success changes the focus from getting approval from others to being happy with your own work, from financial wealth to personal growth, and from competing to working together.

Being open to new ideas about what success means can help us grow as people and learn more about ourselves. Success is, we realize, a journey of self-awareness, personal development, and close personal connection with others rather than a goal.

It's about really living, following our interests, and changing the planet. As we start to define success differently, let's challenge the status quo and look at how social expectations influence our aspirations.

Let's find out for all of us what is most important and make sure our actions align with those values and goals. In its purest form, success is not about moving up the ladder but about living a life with purpose, meaning, and satisfaction.

It's about liking ourselves, recognizing our unique skills, and making other people's lives better. Let us dare to redefine success and start a path of self-discovery, development, and transformation.

CHAPTER 5

Mapping Out Goals

What goals do you have in mind? Many of us believe that we know what we want out of life, but in many situations, we are either thinking too little or we haven't tapped into our subconscious to pursue our true desires that are centered around our basic values.

Take five minutes to listen to a guided meditation that will help you imagine living a limitless, flawless life where you wake up every morning as the perfect version of yourself.

- When you glance out your window, what do you first see?

- Which outfit are you wearing to work?

- What city do you reside in? Is it your current residence, or might it be a new one in another nation?

- What is your route to work? By vehicle, bus, train, or airplane?

- Which vehicle, if it's a car, are you operating? What is the appearance of the car's interior and how does the steering wheel feel?

- What do you do and where is your workplace located?

- What do you do for yourself after work? What are your daily activities?

- Do you feel totally content in your family life?

Once your five minutes are up, return to the present and write down the first ten goals that come to mind. Don't forget to include any of them. You are using this to visualize your dream. But achieving your goals requires more than just dreaming. Even if you are the most gifted person alive, there is very little chance that you will realize all of your potential if you don't prepare ahead of time. It's all about the planning! Therefore, make sure you create a goal plan before you even begin your trip toward your personal ambitions.

A goal map serves as your personal route map. It is a single document that outlines all of your individual goals. Your goals in every aspect of your life—financial, cultural, professional, physical, spiritual, and so forth—are included in a goal map.

Your life's different facets are all interconnected. The two scarce commodities in your life, time and energy, are contested by your hobbies and life goals. You need to think about your life as a whole! The comprehensiveness of a target map is one of its main advantages.

Keep in mind that your time and energy are finite resources, and anything you wish to accomplish will compete for them. You will therefore be able to develop relevant and attainable goals with the aid of the methods highlighted below.

Step 1: Consider and Evaluate

Think back for a moment on the previous six months. What achievements have you made? Have you faced any difficulties? Evaluate your achievements in a number of areas of your life, such as your relationships, career, health, and personal growth. Tell yourself honestly, appreciating your opportunities for growth as well as your accomplishments. You can use this review to help you create goals for the second half of the year.

Step 2: Establish Your Prioritization

It's time to set your priorities now that you have a clearer picture of your situation. You may still be wondering, "What really matters to me?" Consider what fulfills your desires, elevates your standards, and brings you joy. It's important to set goals that align with your own desires and aspirations. Sort them based on significance and how they will impact your life on a personal and professional level.

Step 3: Make SMART objectives

It's time to develop SMART goals- Specific, Measurable, Achievable, Relevant, and Time-bound. Keep your priorities in mind. Steer clear of generalizations like "get healthier" or "advance my career." Rather, define and prioritize your goals. For instance, "Run a 5K race by October," and "Increase sales by 15% by December." Establishing SMART goals helps you maintain focus and gives them a more concrete form.

Your goal map needs to have S.M.A.R.T. goals. A smart objective must be time-bound, relevant, quantifiable, attainable, and detailed.

- **Smart:** You should have certain aims in mind. If there is no bull's-eye, you cannot hit it. Saying "I want to lose 4 kg by year's end" instead of "I want to lose weight" is a better strategy (goal quantity and date are key).

- **Measurable:** Your objectives ought to be measured so that you can determine whether you are on course at any given moment. This will allow you to regularly monitor your progress.

- **Achievable:** Be realistic and avoid over-planning. Your goal ought to be within your grasp. If it's too enormous, try breaking it down into more attainable objectives that you can accomplish gradually.

- **Relevant:** Your objectives should be personally meaningful to you, rooted in your highest hopes, and consistent with your beliefs.

- **Time-bound:** This is a crucial point. Let's get real here: you should have a deadline for your goals. If there isn't a deadline, a goal is merely a wish.

Step 4: Dissect It

Although setting smaller, more doable goals helps make larger goals feel more feasible, large goals might still feel daunting. Break down each objective into manageable steps or benchmarks.

If your objective is to learn a new language, for example, you can divide it up into manageable tasks like signing up for a course, learning vocabulary every day, or locating a language exchange partner. Breaking up your work into smaller tasks will help you feel more motivated as you move forward.

Step 5: Establish a schedule

Give each task or milestone a deadline. A deadline instills a sense of responsibility and urgency. Map out your objectives using a project management application. Recognize the limitations of your time and set priorities appropriately. Always be adaptable because there may be adjustments needed along the way.

Step 6: Monitor Your Development

Keep an eye on your development on a regular basis to stay inspired and make any required corrections. Rejoice in little victories along the road to keep moving forward. To help you stay on track, think about keeping a journal, utilizing an app that tracks your habits, or hiring a coach or accountability partner. Tracking your progress enables you to identify areas that may require additional effort or modification in addition to highlighting your accomplishments.

Step 7: Change and Progress

Situations and priorities might alter as life progresses. Remain flexible and receptive to changes. Check in with your goals from time to time to make sure they still reflect your changing desires. Embrace the opportunity to grow from every challenge you face. Remember that the trip is just as vital as the end point. Remember also that creating goals is a continuous process of personal development and exploration rather than a one-time event.

Recognize the path ahead, maintain focus, and respect each turning point. Through commitment and a clear plan of action, you will optimize your potential and set yourself up for success. When creating a goal map, it can be helpful to consider the following questions: **Why, How, and Who.** This is a practical explanation of how a goal map is drafted.

- **Why**

Determine the emotions that drive you. All thoughts are equal—good and rational thinking until emotions enter the picture, at which point everything else becomes irrelevant. Why can't you just go forward and accomplish your goals without making any justifications or doubts? Perhaps feelings like love, independence, family, development, or contribution might be the cause.

Put your three main arguments in writing at the top of the page, above your objectives. You should also repeat this information in the form of an image. It's time to restore the magic in our lives and commit to a date because, as we've all heard, "A goal without a date is just a wish."

You can't be 20 pounds overweight and have abs in the morning, so strike a balance between bravery and realistic expectations for the time being. Now that you have your success date in your head, it's time to put it on paper. Write your date directly below your goals, then draw a line to the bottom of the page and write today's date. Use that line as a guide to help you remember what needs to be done in the meantime to accomplish your major goal.

- **How**

Identify the steps you must take to get from your current place to your destination, including what you need to learn, study, save, and/or acquire new skills to get there. As you move along the timeline, start with the earliest and end with today's date. Consider this step in relation to any past success we may have had.

There are important steps we must take to succeed, break them down, and always start with the most doable one. Moreover, use one page for text and another for images to engage both sides of the brain, and don't forget to use color.

- **Who**

Select those who will be able to help you. Any worthwhile aim will typically need some help and encouragement, whether from your parents, coach, mentor, or spouse.

Always write the person's name across from the step you need assistance with. Keep in mind the power of association. Since we are the average of the five people we spend the most time with, make sure your life is accelerated by the five important people—in this case, the three crucial people—rather than anchored by them.

Remember this advice at all times when you're considering your objectives **(The 4S system).**

- Sign It: Ensure it's a promise
- Say it: Talk in affirmations
- See it: Visualize it every morning
- Share it: Tell like-minded people about it

So why is a goal plan necessary for everyone?

It's crucial that your goal map be accessible at all times and frequently reviewed. It ought to be a dynamic document that is updated frequently based on your performance and how your priorities change over time. After defining a goal map, let's examine the reasons why you should have one!

1. Take charge of your fate.

You begin to take charge of your future by creating your own goal plan. You are your own programmer; you make the decisions, plan, and carry them out. Since it's YOUR life, you ought to be in charge of it. Make your own decisions and write the narrative rather than just following along.

2. Clearly state your intentions

What is it that you actually desire out of life? Put in the effort to advance professionally or prioritize family time? Can you play the piano? Read each day? You must identify your true motivations and set goals that are consistent with your morals and beliefs. First and foremost, listen to your heart!

You'll quickly find that some of your goals are actually very nebulous when you start delving into the specifics of what you hope to accomplish in life. Ambitious goals are not achievable. One of the key advantages of a goal map is this: It forces you to figure out what matters most to you personally. You know which way to go once you have this clarity. You can begin strolling along that path and monitor your advancement as you go.

3. Set priorities to do more.

As we previously stated, time, energy, and money are the same resources that are needed for all of our desired outcomes. Given the limitations of these resources, we must make decisions. A goal map will guide these decisions for you.

Using a goal map to organize your life journey is similar to using a GPS. Maybe you should tour this country first, then this region, instead of traveling back and forth and burning up fuel. You will ultimately receive nothing if you have too many contradictory desires. You can see a clear picture of your life and spot these conflicts and obstacles by creating a goal map.

It's not just about identifying conflicts; it's also about figuring out how to bring your objectives together and make positive connections between your actions. Participating in sports can improve your stress management and social skills; after a demanding workday, meditation can offer a helpful spiritual respite and improve your cognitive clarity; etc. You can jointly describe these positive loops with the use of a goal map.

4. Be aware of your surroundings

You're going to make future decision-making easier with the help of your action plan. There is a clear course of action, and making decisions is easy: you avoid needless tension. Now that your GPS is configured, just adhere to the directions! It's not necessary for you to constantly be concerned with your location and direction of travel. Simply periodically check your monitor and change the trajectory as necessary.

5. Recognize who you are

Ultimately, this is maybe the most significant: developing a goal map improves your understanding of yourself. It serves as a mirror and a tool for self-communication. What do I plan to do next year? How much work am I willing to put in to achieve my goals? For what reason do I put off doing this one but not that other one? What is truly important to me? What brings me joy?

You can have a profound dialogue with yourself by identifying and honing the goals you wish to pursue. It's a process where you explore and develop your identities. The path to true happiness is this one. One tool that helps you have this conversation with yourself is a goal map. Wisdom is knowledge of others; enlightenment is knowing oneself.

CHAPTER 6

Rewiring The Brain

Neuroplasticity and Development of Habits

Over the last ten years, innovative studies have transformed our comprehension of the human brain. And with all of this new knowledge, we can finally learn how to use our brain power to our advantage. Understanding how your brain functions can give you a significant advantage in your attempts to lead a long, happy, and healthy life. Knowledge truly is power.

To actually make any kind of change, all you really need to do is learn to collaborate with your brain. And you may achieve this by retraining your mind to focus on your own success. Recall that your brain is in charge of assisting you in realizing your aspirations. It is in charge of helping you get over your worries, limiting ideas, and unfavorable self-talk.

Are you prepared to discover how to discipline your thoughts to behave? Let's investigate the marvels of the human brain first. In this manner, you'll be aware of your challenges as you discover how to successfully train your brain. Your flexible mind is flexible enough to adjust. Your brain is always working to make sense of the moment that just ended, seeking to regulate, comprehend, and give meaning to it. We can never stop grabbing hold of what has just passed by.

A popular neuropsychologist and instructor of meditation states that the brain and the mind are one integrated entity. The mind evolves along with the brain. The brain changes in tandem with mental changes. It makes sense. Furthermore, because of your brain's plasticity, you have the ability to permanently alter it for your own happiness and well-being.

What precisely is neuroplasticity, then?

The idea of neuroplasticity—that your brain evolves throughout the course of your lifetime—is supported by neuroscience. It is the phrase used to explain a series of reactions your brain has to external stimuli. To put it another way, your thoughts, feelings, behaviors, and experiences literally alter how your brain works.

Neuroplasticity or brain plasticity is another term for the brain's ABILITY to CHANGE and enable a person to LEARN/RELEARN how to adapt to various situations. This amazing finding enhances focus and emotional responsiveness in stroke, brain damage, learning disability, traumatic event, and depression patients during their recuperation.

The ability of the brain to alter its structure and function in response to our feelings, ideas, and behaviors is a relatively new subject of discussion among neuroscientists and neuropsychologists.

A revolution in brain plasticity is happening right now. The first step toward that revolution is realizing that, during the course of your natural life, your brain is constantly being rewired and functionally altered, largely under your control. At any age, you possess an amazing innate capacity to enhance and develop who you are.

The majority of scientists held the belief that the adult brain was inflexible and hardwired in the preceding ten years. This is however not the case. You have the superpower of neuroplasticity, which you can utilize to mold your reality. Quite radical, you would think.

Whether you realize it or not, neuroplasticity is a constant occurrence that occurs throughout the day. Nonetheless, you have the ability to access the creative portion of your brain and deliberately decide how to take advantage of neuroplasticity. Anyone, including those who have never experienced trauma or brain injury, can benefit from neuroplasticity by learning to have greater mental control over their lives.

In fact, a clinical professor's research demonstrated how neuroplasticity might be used for personal empowerment through therapy and brain function growth. And adopting a better lifestyle and shifting your priorities will make this feasible.

This is the situation. Your brain releases the chemicals and hormones necessary for mental transformation when you're feeling inspired, aware, and prepared to act. Your switches for change, however, go off when you're preoccupied, uninterested, or engaged in unimportant tasks that don't require your full attention.

Our brains get hardwired with our routines, behaviors, and addictions (e.g., smoking a cigarette, checking your phone while your hands are idle, or enjoying a few glasses of wine to relax after work), which reinforces the neural pathways associated with this kind of behavior.

Furthermore, tension and worry over events from the past or things we believe may happen in the future, as well as our typical responses to others and ourselves, are all components of our neuroplastic makeup.

Your brain and mind will continue to support and promote the things you consistently perform; this is no longer a mystery. The strength of the brain connections increases with practice or rehearsal. Thus, consider the following: Which behaviors do I wish to support? What goals do I have for my lifetime?

After you've written down the solutions, the following stage is to teach your brain to operate accordingly so that you can take decisive action to realize your aspirations and goals. The development of new skills and the reinforcement of desired behavior lead to anatomical and functional changes in our brains. It really is that easy. Rewiring your brain for success just requires a great deal of work and dedication. But don't you think it's worth it?

Your brain is able to develop and change for the better. You may live a better, wealthier, and happier life at any age by continuing to learn, grow, and hone your abilities. Your mind changes when your brain changes, and you may alter your life by altering your mind.

It is possible to make tiny mental adjustments that have a big impact on your brain and life experiences as a whole. You have the ability to rewire your brain to pursue your desires.

How might neuroplasticity be enhanced?

Discovering your basic beliefs will help your brain develop. Clear your head and make room for fresh ideas. Consider this:

- What motivates you?
- Which interests do you have?
- Which qualities do you possess?
- What are the priorities in your life?

Think about your current circumstances and your goals while you reflect and meditate. You can begin to align your other plans after you have a clear understanding of your key principles.

Also, make goals that will inspire you. After you have a clear understanding of your basic beliefs, you will achieve your goals. Setting attainable yet significant goals increases your motivation to reach them, even if the bar is set excessively high.

Remember to take it step by step if you want to escape the overpowering feeling that comes with change. This is because it's easier to start small, finish easy every day, and then monitor your development. You'll be shocked at how far you've gone.

The following are some essential pointers to enhance neuroplasticity:

- **Work out.**

For a healthier brain, you can improve neuroplasticity at home with a few simple activities. Exercise promotes better cognitive function, which in turn improves brain health. Any physical activity that benefits the heart also benefits the brain. This is due to the fact that an elevated heart rate causes your brain to receive more oxygen, which nourishes and encourages the formation of new brain cells. Exercise also enhances memory function and reaction time.

Engaging in any physical activity first thing in the morning can help you become ready for emotional stress. This is because when we exercise, our brain releases endorphins, a chemical that makes us feel good.

- **Appropriate diet.**

Food, as we all know, provides us with energy, and eating a good, balanced diet helps our brains work properly. Certain foods that improve brain function typically include omega-3 fatty acids, B vitamins, and antioxidants.

Providing your body with the proper nutrients will also affect the overall health, lifespan, and function of your brain. Reducing your intake of sugar-filled drinks, such sodas, can raise your risk of developing diabetes as well as worsening or possibly completely losing your memory. Foods heavy in trans fats, alcohol, refined carbs, aspartame (an artificial sweetener), and highly processed foods should also be avoided.

- **Rest**

The human brain requires sleep to function properly. Studies demonstrate that sleep deprivation impairs memory and learning, which lowers brain function. Sleep is just as vital to your brain's optimal functioning as food and oxygen are. On the flip side, since your body and brain won't work properly, getting too little sleep will reduce your quality of life.

- **Rewire your brain to overcome stress**

Stress originates from our negative reactions to circumstances. Although there are many reasons for stress, issues and worries regarding one's health, finances, family, and employment are the most prevalent ones. It may also be long-term or short-term.

However, long-term stress leads to an accumulation of cortisol, our main stress hormone, in our bodies, which ages and damages the brain. This leads to abnormal brain function, which shrinks the brain and causes brain cell death. It would be simpler for you to get clarity on your goals and the reasons behind them if you implemented these new lifestyle adjustments.

- **Decide who your influences and circle are.**

Increase the amount of time you spend with others who inspire and encourage you and, to the greatest extent feasible, who share your basic beliefs. When you associate with those kinds of individuals, your neuroplasticity rises and a meaningful growth attitude is created.

- **Don't put off doing it.**

You will not get anywhere by procrastinating, and it will not enhance your brain's adaptability. Through mindfulness practice, you can break free from that negative habit. You do this by keeping yourself and those around you aware of what is going on. You may make the most of your time and develop value-based resolutions if you are observant of your surroundings, your thoughts, and your state of mind.

It's never too late to make changes in your life. You still have the freedom to live your life as you see fit. You can replace your negative, outdated behaviors with positive ones. Enhance neuroplasticity to begin reprogramming your brain right away.

CHAPTER 7

Fostering A Growth Mindset

We all gloat over the accomplishments of others and celebrate our own wins. However, we seldom ever recognize that failures frequently open the door to achievement. We fear the process that will lead us to achievement, but we seek success because our attention is fixed on shining successes. It's absurd to think you can win everything and never lose. Examine these notable examples of "successful failures".

The first black billionaire in history and most famous television host, Oprah Winfrey, lost her job as a Baltimore TV anchor. She was deemed "unfit for television" by the producer.

Among the most successful animators of all time, Walt Disney was let go from one of his first positions at the Kansas City Star due to the editor's criticism that he "lacked imagination and had no good ideas."

Stephen King, the King of Horror, almost gave up on writing after thirty publishers rejected his novel "Carrie". King threw the manuscript in the bin, but his wife found it and begged him to give it another shot. After the release of Carrie, King cemented his reputation as one of the best horror writers of all time.

How, then, did their setbacks eventually contribute to their success? It all boils down to attitude. A well-known academic psychologist has studied attitude and how it affects motivation, self-control, and achievement. She distinguishes between fixed and development mindsets, emphasizing the differences in how we respond to failure. However, let's clarify what we mean by "mindset" before delving into growth and fixed mindsets.

What "mindset" means

A person's mindset is made up of a collection of strongly held, influential ideas that influence how they see the world and themselves. It serves as a framework for both work and life, providing a perspective on opportunities and your capacity for overcoming obstacles. Your mindset greatly influences how you view success and failure in life.

It's critical to understand that your self-perception has a significant impact on how you live. It can decide whether you grow into the person you want to be and whether you achieve the goals that are important to you.

By growth and fixed attitude, what do we mean?

The idea that your intelligence, abilities, and skills are innate and unchangeable is known as a fixed mindset. No matter how hard you try, you can't really control them. In this sense, your potential is determined by the hand you are dealt in life.

The idea that your intelligence, abilities, and skills are changeable and can be developed with time, effort, and practice is known as a growth mindset. It acknowledges that although everyone of us has unique skills and passions, we can all get better.

Comparison of Growth and Fixed Mindsets in Relation to Success and Failure

Based on their respective sets of ideas, growth and fixed mindsets take quite different approaches to success and failure.

1. Unchanging Mentality

- Success:

The idea that abilities are innate and unchangeable puts pressure on someone with a fixed mindset to "prove" themselves. Achievement and success serve as validation of preexisting skills. People who have a fixed mindset focus all of their energy on ways to prove they are "better" than other people.

- Failure:

A person with a fixed mindset responds defensively and competitively out of insecurity, trying to justify their "natural" talents. They have to defend themselves against the threat of failure. Errors reveal shortcomings, and shortcomings are proof of one's own insufficiency. People with a fixed attitude ignore criticism and place the blame elsewhere, never learning from their mistakes. Failure in a fixed mindset is equivalent to;

1. "My capabilities end in failure."
2. "It's either me or it's not me."
3. "When I become frustrated, I give up."

This kind of thinking prevents advancement by shielding the individual from obstacles that can promote development and creating a strong dread of failing.

2. Growth-oriented Thinking

- Success:

In a development mentality, advancement takes precedence above success. A person with a growth mentality values the effort they put in and the landmarks they reach along the way rather than concentrating on the end goal. They understand that success is only a byproduct of these efforts; learning and progress are the results of perseverance and hard work. A person with a growth mentality is driven by internal motivation and isn't worried about getting approval from others.

- Failure:

A person with a development mindset views failure as a teaching opportunity rather than a flaw. Making errors enables people to learn more as it is a necessary component of the discovery process. Individuals that possess a development mentality accept responsibility for their mistakes and proceed, understanding that learning does not equate to failure. This is because curiosity drives people forward, they are more open to trying new things when they have this mindset. We value constructive criticism and feedback as important resources.

How to Develop a Growth Mentality

Because it helps you to go outside of your comfort zone, learn from your mistakes, and persevere through failures, a growth mindset is favorable to success. Although developing a growth mindset requires intentionality, the rewards eventually include increased drive, success, and happiness. There are several methods you can use to start cultivating a growth mindset:

- Determine situations you have a fixed mindset in

You most likely have a growth mindset in certain situations and a fixed attitude in others, thus your mindset isn't constant. Look for instances when you prefer to avoid or give up on things you know are healthy for you in order to determine whether you have a stuck attitude. Boredom, worry, and discomfort are also indicators of things you consider to be fixed.

- Ask for comments

Acknowledge that there are people who can improve you; after all, it's not feasible to think you can achieve perfection in every aspect of your life or career. Don't be scared to ask others where you might improve;

constructive criticism is a great tool for identifying blind spots.

- Accept failure

It's acceptable for you to make mistakes; they will happen. Accept responsibility for your mistakes. You deprive yourself of the chance to make things right when you place the blame elsewhere or assign blame to other factors. Become inquisitive following an error. "What obstacles kept me from achieving my goal?" Ask yourself.

- Go for difficulties

Taking on tasks that require you to use your full skill set is a terrific way to develop and get ready for bigger opportunities down the road. Never turn down an opportunity because you don't think you have the necessary abilities in place. Change the way you perceive obstacles by viewing them as an opportunity, a test, or an adventure.

- Make inquiries

Make the most of people's knowledge by posing inquiries. None of us understands everything, after all. Get curious about things instead of being afraid or ashamed of your ignorance! If you're worried about coming across as foolish, keep in mind that your inner critic is more judgmental than those around you.

- Enjoy the adventure with pride

Prioritize your progress over your outcomes. You miss out on the opportunities to learn along the road when you become too focused on the destination. Not success is the goal; learning and development are.

- Honor effort rather than talent

Focusing on your current skills means you're thinking about them in a stagnant manner. Rather, acknowledge and appreciate your efforts and your growing ability to acquire new knowledge and abilities.

- Make use of the "yet" power.

Are you having trouble completing a task or reaching a goal? Remember that you are not an expert at it "yet." Using the word "yet" to reframe the difficulty creates opportunity and serves as a reminder that you can still advance in spite of obstacles.

BEYOND THE REGULAR

Daring to go beyond the norms take you to heights yet unseen ~ Elsie Gabe

CHAPTER 8

Morning Visualization

Thinking back on successes and optimism, for most of us, thinking back on our accomplishments is not a natural trait. Usually, the hectic pace of the holidays, work, family, and other obligations take precedence.

Ever had the impression that life was happening automatically? Indeed, I have. I can occasionally become so engrossed in my routine that I forget what I have done in a given year. It seems like I blink, and then December rolls along and another year has gone by. In self-reflection, we analyze and consider our ideas, deeds, emotions, and experiences. It facilitates self-understanding and personal development and can be achieved in a number of methods, such as through writing, meditation, and asking close friends and family for input.

Setting the tone for the day and bringing ourselves in line with our dreams and ambitions should happen at the hallowed hour of the morning. Establishing a morning visualization routine is a highly effective way to foster an optimistic, introspective, and purposeful mindset.

For me, keeping a journal helps me stay accountable for my progress toward my objectives. It enables me to take a break, consider my accomplishments for the year, and give thanks to people who have supported me throughout difficult times. Every obstacle presents an opportunity for development and self-awareness. Take forth the knowledge you've gained and your accomplishments.

The Influence of Introspection

Thinking back on our accomplishments is a purposeful process that helps us understand our journey better than simply taking a quick look at them. Here are a few viewpoints on the importance of self-reflection:

- Personal Development and Learning:

Self-reflection gives us the chance to draw lessons from our past. Making sense of what went well and what didn't allows us to make better judgments in the future.

As an illustration, let's say you finished a difficult job at work. By thinking back on the procedure, you can pinpoint the tactics that worked and where you still need to make improvements.

- Gratitude and Appreciation:

Taking the time to acknowledge our successes helps us feel grateful. It serves as a reminder of our accomplishments and the work we've put in. For instance, you might think back on your late-night study sessions, encouraging friends, and personal perseverance after acing a challenging exam.

- Increasing Confidence:

Thinking back on our prior successes helps us feel more confident. It serves as a reminder that we are able to overcome challenges. A musician thinking back on their very first public performance may remember how anxious they were at first and how they overcame it.

Techniques for Efficient Introspection

Let's now examine several doable strategies for conducting insightful introspection:

- Writing in a Journal:

Keep a thoughtful notebook in which you record your successes, setbacks, and emotions related to them. Write, for instance, about the satisfaction you had after finishing a marathon or the things you took away from a botched business endeavor.

- Set Aside Dedicated Time:

Make time each day for introspection. It could occur every week, every month, or following important benchmarks. You can take thirty minutes each Sunday night to reflect on your week's successes and areas for growth.

- Pose Intriguing Questions:

Think about asking yourself:
- What did I accomplish today, this week, or this month?
- What challenges did I surmount?
- In what ways did I help others succeed?

Consider, for instance, how your team benefited from your leadership during a cooperative effort.

Honoring Your Successes

Enjoyment is a crucial step in the procedure. Here's how you can commemorate your successes:

I. Small Wins Matter: Honour every accomplishment, no matter how tiny. It may be putting an end to a book, working out, or preparing a new dish. Also, after finishing a difficult task at work, you can reward yourself with your favorite dessert.

II. Share with Others: Let your friends, family, and coworkers know about your accomplishments so that you may all celebrate together. You can throw a little party for your team when a product launch goes well.

III. Make Rituals: Establish customs that are unique for commemorating anniversaries. It might be going on a solitary hike, penning a note of gratitude to oneself, or lighting a candle. For example as a thank you for your hard work, give yourself a spa day on your anniversary of employment each year.

Best Practices For A Morning Visualization Ritual

1. Allocate specific time: Set aside a certain amount of time every morning to engage in your visualization practice, ideally before you begin your day activities. Select a calm, serene setting where you may unwind and concentrate without interruptions.

2. Write a visualization script: Write a mental storyboard or script that includes information, feelings, and sensory sensations for your visualization. Imagine yourself accomplishing your objectives, getting past challenges, and feeling happy and content.

3. Use all of your senses: Using all of your senses can help your visualization come to life. Visualize the sights, sounds, tastes, smells, and textures that are connected to the results you want to achieve. This will help you create a vivid and engaging experience.

4. Express gratitude: To start your visualization practice, take a moment to express your gratitude for all of life's blessings and accomplishments. Cultivate an attitude of appreciation and abundance by expressing gratitude for the chances, resources, and richness that are all around you.

5. Remain open and responsive: Throughout the visualization routine, keep your mind open and responsive to any insights, ideas, or direction that may come to you. Put your faith in your inner knowledge and intuition, and let them lead you to your fullest potential.

Thinking back on your accomplishments is more than just giving yourself a pat on the back; it's also a chance to develop, learn, and cherish the experience. So, today, take a moment to recognize and celebrate your accomplishments in a way that is special to you.

The Value of a Daily Visualization Practice

A morning visualization routine has many advantages for our mental, emotional, and spiritual well-being. It is the foundation of personal development and wellbeing. Why you should make this a daily practice, isn't far-fetched.

- Sets a great Tone for the Day:

Visualization exercises in the morning instill optimism, thankfulness, and enthusiasm in your mind and soul, setting a great tone for the day. By visualizing your objectives, successes, and blessings, you create a feeling of possibility and abundance that gets you through the day.

- Improves Focus and Clarity:

Setting priorities and concentrating on what really matters are made easier by visualizing your objectives and dreams. You may prepare your mind for success and give yourself the confidence to take deliberate action toward your goals by mentally practicing the results you want.

- Increases Self-Efficacy and Confidence:

Practicing morning visualization increases your self-efficacy and self-belief. You may increase your self-efficacy and confidence, which will enable you to face challenges head-on with resiliency and commitment. Visualize yourself conquering barriers and reaching your goals.

- Encourages Gratitude and Appreciation:

Thinking back on your successes and blessings helps you feel deeply appreciative of the wealth in your life. Recognizing your accomplishments and the benefits you've been given helps you develop a positive outlook that draws additional possibilities and blessings into your life.

- Aligns Mind, Body, and Spirit:

By promoting harmony and balance in your life, a morning visualization practice aligns your mind, body, and spirit. You can access a source of inspiration and direction that propels your path towards purpose and satisfaction by connecting with your deepest ambitions and aspirations.

Beyond Regular Habits

CHAPTER 9

Reflective Journaling

Keeping a journal or notebook on a regular basis to document your ideas, experiences, and insights is a beneficial practice known as reflective journaling. It is a tool for introspection, self-reflection, and personal development. Well done, you've accomplished one of your main objectives! How can you maximize the benefits of that accomplishment? Consider what you've accomplished!

Use these four thoughtful writing exercises to acknowledge your efforts, praise your development, and get you closer to your objectives.

1. "How satisfied am I with this accomplishment?"

"How satisfied am I with this accomplishment?" Ask yourself. How satisfied or proud you are with your work is what defines satisfaction. Consider how pleased you are with your accomplishment. A tennis player expresses, "I hope I can continue to be happy." However, as you can see, I'm working really hard.

Be truthful in your feelings and opinions. You are more likely to be happy with your achievement if you put in a lot of time and effort. If you believe you could have done more, use that mindset to spur you on to accomplish your next objectives.

Activity: Use a number scale from 1 to 10 to indicate your level of satisfaction with your accomplishment in a few phrases. Explain the what, how, and why to back up your emotions.

Were you aware? Maintaining a record of your achievements helps you articulate your goals and enhances your sense of self-worth. When writing resumes for employers, this is helpful because it will showcase you as an excellent applicant!

2. "What challenges did I overcome?"

It feels good to accomplish something since it means you conquered a challenge. Thinking about your resilience and problem-solving abilities can be achieved by asking oneself, "What challenges did I overcome?"

No task is too big or too little. It could be analyzed based on:
- Beliefs: An attitude that restricts your potential
- Ability: Feats you previously believed were impossible
- Difficulty: A difficulty is a complicated circumstance or challenge.
- Opportunity: The necessity to look for other solutions to an issue
- Cooperation: Collaborating with or without other people

Thinking back on the obstacles you overcome can help you feel better about yourself and more satisfied with your overall performance. As you witness your own accomplishments, you gain self-assurance to take on more challenging tasks in the future.

Activity: Identify a hurdle you overcome to accomplish your objective. Explain the circumstances, the actions you took to resolve them, and how they contributed to your success.

3. "What did I learn?"

Your success resulted from a path of learning. "What did I learn from this experience?" is a question that would help you know and apply methods to future objectives. You might discuss your own development or the new abilities and knowledge you have acquired.

Consider this:

-Who gave you support? ("__ supported me by...")
-What steps did you perform? ("I learned that doing __ can...")
-What tactics or tools did you employ? ("I did it by__ which...")
-What should you steer clear of going forward? ("I learned that __ is not helpful because...")
-How have I changed personally? ("I learned that I...")

4. "What is my next big accomplishment?"

Consider your next objective when you set yourself up for success. "What is my next big accomplishment?" This objective may be long-term or short-term in nature.

- Objectives that can be completed in a few months or a year (getting a job) are examples of short-term goals.
- Making baby steps or progress toward a bigger objective (saving $100 monthly)

- Single circumstances (passing a challenging class by performing well on tests)

Among the long-term objectives are those that may need years of preparation and planning (such as purchasing a home).
- Short-term objectives to attain the main objective (graduating via passing classes)
- Your goals for the future, such as pursuing a lucrative profession as a doctor

You can put the knowledge and abilities you gained from your most recent triumph to use by planning your future achievements. Write down your thoughts to make your goal of becoming the next big thing more definite. Make use of the knowledge you have gained to formulate concrete actions that will enable you to accomplish your new objective.

Act Now! With these journaling questions, let your successes motivate you to take on the next big project. Acknowledging and appreciating your progress can start a positive feedback loop that will motivate you to keep going and achieve more!

Maximize the value of your accomplishments by:

- Grading how satisfied you are with the accomplishment
- Considering the difficulties you overcome
- Noting the lessons you took away from the encounter
- Creating a plan of action for your next objective

Why is Reflective Journaling Important?

Many advantages of reflective journaling support both professional and personal achievement. This is why it is imperative that you make this a daily practice:

1. Make Goals and Priorities Clear: Reflective journaling gives you a place to make your values, priorities, and goals more apparent. Writing out your goals and intentions gives you concentration and clarity, which makes it easier to match your activities to your overall goals.

2. Encourages Self-Awareness as well as Emotional Intelligence: Reflective journaling pushes you to go deeply into your ideas, emotions, and reactions, which helps you become more self-aware and emotionally intelligent. Gaining an objective viewpoint allows you to analyze your experiences and identify your motives, areas of strength, and room for improvement.

3. Supports Decision-Making and Problem-Solving: Reflective journaling is an effective tool for decision-making and problem-solving. Writing down your difficulties, failures, and accomplishments gives you insight into recurring trends and possible solutions, enabling you to make wise decisions and overcome roadblocks.

4. Promotes Learning and Growth: By pushing you to think back on your experiences, draw lessons from them, and pinpoint areas that need work, reflective journaling promotes lifelong learning and personal development. You build a knowledge base that guides your future choices and activities by recording your realizations and insights.

5. Develops Gratitude and Resilience: Reflective journaling helps you develop resilience and gratitude by encouraging you to recognize and value the blessings in your life, despite obstacles or disappointments. By concentrating on these positive experiences, you change your perspective from one of scarcity to one of abundance, which promotes a positive outlook and mindset.

Advice on Writing Reflective Journals That Work

- Set Aside Dedicated Time:

Make sure your daily or weekly schedule includes regular times for introspective journaling. Select a peaceful, quiet space where you may concentrate and reflect without interruptions.

- Be Honest and Authentic:

Embrace vulnerability and self-disclosure as catalysts for growth and self-discovery. Approach reflective writing with honesty and authenticity, allowing yourself to communicate your ideas, feelings, and experiences openly and frankly.

- Use Prompting Thoughts:

When journaling, use questions that provoke thought as a way to encourage reflection and investigation. Examples of such questions include: "What have I learnt today?", "What challenges did I encounter?", and "What am I grateful for?" In your journaling practice, give careful thought to the victories and setbacks you have experienced. Acknowledge and celebrate your accomplishments, as well as the lessons you have learned from obstacles and mistakes.

- Review and Reflect Often:

Go back over your reflective diary entries from time to time to see how you're doing, see any themes or patterns that keep coming up, and gauge your overall improvement. Going forward, make use of these insights to improve your objectives, plans of action, and tactics. Reflective journaling is a life-changing technique that enables people to develop self-awareness, define their objectives, and travel intentionally and purposefully toward success and achievement.

On your own, you can discover the potential for significant personal and professional growth, resilience, and fulfillment when you put this practice into your daily routine and accept the process of self-reflection and introspection. Reflective journaling is very powerful. Accept it today and see how it helps you achieve your goals and reach your maximum potential.

CHAPTER 10

Digital Detox

It might be simple to feel as though we are never really alone in the digitally linked world of today. There is always someone or something fighting for our attention because social media is always present and because there are so many gadgets that allow us to be online all the time. It's important to keep in mind the importance of learning how to be alone, even with all the advantages of being connected.

One benefit of solitude is that it helps us unwind and rejuvenate. We will be able to turn within and detach from the outside world's constant stimulation, which will allow us to ponder and work through our feelings and ideas.

It is simple to become engrossed in the commotion of today's fast-paced world and forget what truly matters to us. We can refocus and recenter ourselves by spending some time alone. This enables us to return to our everyday lives with fresh clarity and purpose.

Furthermore, there are moments when being at ease and by ourselves can strengthen our bonds with other people. It can assist us in more clearly understanding our needs and boundaries and in effectively communicating them to others. Additionally, it can help us become more self-sufficient and independent, which can be desirable traits in a friend or lover.

We rely on other people for approval and support far too frequently, yet developing our ability to be by ourselves can make us more self-assured and independent. Because we can bring our best selves to the table instead of depending on others to fill a hole, this can result in healthier, more rewarding relationships with others.

However, the advantages of solitude extend beyond our private life; it can also enhance our inventiveness and efficiency. We are better able to concentrate on our work and generate fresh ideas when there are no outside interruptions. It's simple to fall victim to groupthink, but spending time by ourselves frees our minds to think creatively and independently. This can be especially helpful in the workplace, where coming up with creative solutions to issues is frequently required.

Being by ourselves can be challenging at times, particularly if we are not accustomed to it. It can be frightening to face our feelings and thoughts, and we may be tempted to use technology or other forms of diversion to pass the time when there is stillness.

On the other hand, discovering contentment in solitude can be a rewarding journey. It can lead to greater fulfillment and happiness in both our personal and professional life by helping us understand ourselves, our beliefs, and our goals better.

It is more crucial than ever to take care of ourselves and develop our ability to be at ease in our own company in today's constantly connected society. Thus, don't be scared to disconnect and get some alone time. Although at first it could seem scary, the advantages are priceless. It can be a quiet evening at home, a single trip, or just a few minutes alone in a park, but it can aid in our self-reconnection and help us discover deeper purpose in life.

Here are five simple steps you may take to prepare for a digital detox:

1. Limit the amount of time you spend on your devices:

Restricting the amount of time you spend on your gadgets each day is a simple approach to begin a digital detox. To monitor your usage, you can use a third-party app or the built-in screen time tools on your phone or tablet. By putting restrictions on your device usage, you can make sure that you only use it for brief periods of time.

2. Take regular breaks from social media:

Relentlessly avoiding social media is another easy approach to cleanse your system. Just blocking off a few hours, or even a whole day, every week to avoid social media and other internet platforms, can do this.

3. Unplug before going to bed:

This is advisable because the blue light that screens emit might interfere with our sleep cycles and make it more difficult to get to sleep and remain asleep. You should think about unplugging from all screens at least an hour before bed to enhance the quality of your sleep.

4. Establish a screen-free zone:

Choose a particular space in your house, like the living room or bedroom, to be a screen-free zone. This might help you distinguish between your online and offline lives and provide you with a space to unwind and get away from technology.

5. Locate offline interests and activities:

Lastly, think about locating interests and pursuits that don't involve technology. This can be anything from cooking or practicing an instrument to reading a book or taking a stroll. By taking part in offline activities, you can break away from the digital world and lessen your need for technology.

One excellent method to disconnect and rejuvenate is to embark on a digital fast. My use of technology can be better balanced and I can spend more time away from the digital world.

This is easily done by following the steps above; establishing screen-free zones, discovering offline hobbies and activities, unplugging before bed, placing limitations on device usage, and taking breaks from social media.

I've been able to re-establish a connection with myself and my environment by doing these easy activities, which have also helped me feel more focused and present in my daily life. I advise trying a digital detox and observing its advantages.

CHAPTER 11

Time Mastery

Eliminating Procrastination

Why does procrastination impact so many individuals and how can it be overcome? Contrary to popular belief, most individuals do not necessarily view procrastination as a sign of laziness.

In reality, when we wait, we usually put in a lot of extra effort for long stretches of time immediately before our deadlines. Working long hours and hard cannot make us lazy; in fact, the opposite of lazy is true. What can we do to stop ourselves, and more importantly, why do we put things off?

As was previously noted, some people argue that they procrastinate because they are lazy. Some claim they "do better" when things are delayed and they "work best" under duress. I encourage you to think critically about these justifications.

Nearly all of the people who make this claim have a history of delaying important school assignments that they had organized, completed, had time to evaluate, etc., before the due date. As such, individuals are unable to compare the circumstances in which they function at their best.

If you almost always put things off and hardly ever really approach your tasks strategically, you can't really say that you "do better" under pressure. Some people continue to assert that they relish the "rush" of completing assignments on time.

But when they are running behind schedule, this is often what they remark. They assert that this is effective both before and after cramming, when they have forgotten the negative consequences of delaying, such as fatigue, disappointment at not meeting their own standards, and strain and worry from having to put their lives on hold for long stretches of time.

Not to mention that leaving it till the last minute increases the probability that something will go wrong and you won't get the grade you want—like getting sick or having a computer problem. Consequently, we procrastinate despite the fact that it can be harmful to us and increase our likelihood of failing. For what reason is that the case?

Procrastination is not solely the product of poor time management skills; it can also have deeper, more complex psychological roots. These dynamics can be made worse by schools that often assess their pupils, especially in higher education where performance can have a big influence and grades are crucial.

In reality, procrastination is a common defensive tactic used by pupils. For example, if you put things off, you'll always be able to blame your failure on "not having enough" time, so you'll never have to question your skills.

Given the pressure students experience to do well on tasks, such as papers, it is understandable that they would rather avoid it and put off finishing their work. Most of the time, anxiety and fear drive our avoidance and delay behaviors: anxiety about performing too well, anxiety about performing too poorly, concern about losing control, anxiety about being foolish, anxiety about having one's identity or self-concept questioned. To avoid having our abilities criticized, we put off working. Furthermore, performing successfully helps us feel "smarter."

So what can we do to counteract our inclination to put things off?

- Being Aware: Making the First Move

Understanding the REASONS WHY you put things off and the function it serves in your life is the first step towards beating procrastination. You can't create a practical solution if you don't fully understand the cause of the problem. Awareness and self-awareness are key to learning how to stop procrastinating, just like they are for other problems.

Many people find that they can overcome their procrastination issues by understanding how procrastination protects them from feeling inadequate and remembering this when they are tempted to revert to old, unproductive practices of delay. Knowing the true causes makes it easier to stop postponing.

- Time Management: One Piece of the Puzzle

Overcoming procrastination requires time management techniques and tools. But they are insufficient on their own. Moreover, not every time management strategy tackles procrastination in the same way. While certain time management techniques can assist combat procrastination, others might even exacerbate it. The most successful ones are those that reduce worry and fear while emphasizing the advantages and fulfillment of completing tasks.

Individuals that are inflexible, exaggerate the magnitude of their work, and incite anxiety can actually cause you to put things off longer, which is detrimental. For example, creating a big list of "things to do" or scheduling every second of your day may cause tension and delay. Rather, create a reasonable to-do list, divide big tasks into smaller ones, allow yourself some wiggle room, and use leisure time to engage in enjoyable activities as a reward for completing tasks.

- Motivation: Keep Pushing

This is by seeking valuable excuses to engage in tasks. The key to beating procrastination is to keep your motivation high for PRODUCTIVE REASONS. When I refer to "productive reasons," I mean drives to acquire knowledge and accomplish objectives that produce positive, gratifying feelings and actions.

These are not the same as taking on a task because you're afraid you won't succeed, or because you don't want to upset your parents, look silly, or outshine others to "show off." These are all good reasons to act, often very strong ones, but they are all ineffectual because they produce negative, harmful thoughts, feelings, and actions.

For example, you might not attempt new things, ask questions, explore new regions, or take the required risks to learn new things and achieve new heights if you're worried about appearing foolish.

Establishing and concentrating on your goals is a smart method to start positive motivations. Determine your own motivations for taking the course, put them in writing, and use a goal-setting chart to track your advancement. Recall to concentrate on your objectives and motivations. Your goals are obligations to other people; they are not goals at all.

- Maintaining Motivation: Stay Active

Maintaining an active participation in your classes is another way to beat procrastination. Your drive will be weakened if you are a passive student because you are probably not "getting into" the course and its themes. Furthermore, you are probably not getting the most out of the course and its materials if you are passive.

In fact, nonsense and misunderstanding are boring and frustrating rather than interesting. Boring and frustrating tasks are rarely what we want to do. Avoid that by making an effort to comprehend the course material thoroughly rather than just remember it or "get through it."

Alternatively, consider (1) looking for content in the course materials that interests and speaks to you, (2) making a goal for each reading and class, and (3) asking questions about the information you are learning of both yourself and other people.

An overview of strategies for conquering procrastination

- **Awareness:** Consider the causes of your procrastination, as well as the behaviors and ideas that encourage it.

- **Evaluate:** What emotions trigger procrastination, and what emotions result from it? Do you wish to alter these feelings, if they are constructive and positive?

- **Outlook:** Modify your viewpoint. When a large work is broken down into smaller components, it becomes less daunting. Consider the positive aspects of an assignment or the outcomes you hope to achieve in addition to the grade.

- Commit: If you're feeling stuck, just make a simple commitment to finish any task—no matter how small—and put it in writing. When you're done, treat yourself. Only include tasks that you can fully commit to on your schedule or "to do" list, and if you do so, make sure you follow through on them.

By doing this, you will gradually restore the confidence that so many people who put things off have lost—the confidence that you will follow through on your commitments.

- Surroundings: Be selective about who and where you work when conducting schoolwork. Procrastination is the practice of repeatedly putting yourself in settings where you don't get much done, including "studying" in bed, at a coffee shop, or with friends. This can actually be a strategy for avoiding work.

- Goals: Pay attention to what you want to accomplish rather than what you want to avoid. By giving oneself constructive, measurable, and significant learning and accomplishment objectives, you may focus on the beneficial reasons for completing tasks.

- **Be Realistic:** It takes time and work to change habits and achieve goals. Don't set yourself back by having unachievable expectations that you won't be able to fulfill.

- **Self-talk:** Take note of your thoughts and the language you use with yourself. Engage in self-talk that reaffirms your objectives and replaces outdated, unhelpful patterns of self-talk. Say "I will..." rather than "I wish I hadn't..."

- **Un-schedule:** If you're feeling stuck, you won't likely follow a plan that's all work and no play and serves as a continual reminder of everything you need to accomplish.

Create a flexible, loosely structured schedule and only include the things that are absolutely important. Track the time you spend achieving your objectives and treat yourself when you do. By doing this, you may feel less overwhelmed and more satisfied with the work you accomplish.

- **Swiss Cheese It:** Dividing large jobs into smaller ones is a sensible strategy. An alternative approach to this is setting up brief intervals of time for a large work and doing as much as you can during that period with minimal anticipation of the results.

Try, for instance, just writing down any thoughts you have for a paper for ten minutes or scanning a lengthy reading to extract the essential points. When you repeat this process on a large assignment multiple times, you will have gained some momentum, made some headway, and the task will appear less overwhelming because you have already poked holes in it (much like Swiss cheese). To put it briefly, now that you've started and eliminated some of the roadblocks, it will be simpler to accomplish the assignment.

Once procrastination is conquered, improved time management can be attained. And increased efficiency and production will undoubtedly result from this.

CHAPTER 12

Leveraging Social Support

Having a social support system is essential for teaching your objectives. Famously, Arnold Schwarzenegger expressed his belief that the idea of a self-made guy is unreal. During his speech at the University of Houston, he said, "Without my parents, mentors, and teachers, I wouldn't be here."

Building a social support network offers many mental and physical advantages. It has been demonstrated that supportive actions improve long-term mental health by lowering stress and isolating sentiments. Even if these advantages seem obvious, how exactly can having a social support system help in goal-setting? Moreover, how can you make the most of this assistance to become ultimately more effective and productive?

A Social Support Network: What is it?

Establishing a support system of individuals who can offer direction and help is essential to reaching your objectives. Working hard on one's own is quite challenging, and tackling challenging projects will always need a lot of hard work. The greater your aspirations, the more social support you will eventually require for achievement.

Consider the effort difference between developing a great firm and finishing a single job at work. Although one of these things can be the aim, the amount of work needed for each is very different. Consider the difficulty differential between doing your first muscle-up and earning a spot in the CrossFit Games to put this into perspective in terms of fitness. The latter, as you might see, is nearly hard to accomplish on your own and calls for a much wider support system.

A support network should not be mistaken for a support group. Typically, a support group is established to deal with a crisis or to offer a community for people to overcome harmful behavior. These include support groups for addiction, eating disorders, and other issues.

In contrast, a support network is a group of relatives, friends, peers, and mentors who offer support and enrich your life. In times when you might be lost or bewildered on your journey, they can help provide direction and strengthen your resolve by providing counsel, physical resources, perspective, and feedback. Additional benefits of support networks include a greater sense of security, worth, and belonging.

Types of Social Support

Four main types of social support exist, and each is exhibited by a distinct kind of individual in your support system:

- Emotional Support

These are displays of compassion, love, trust, and empathy. You personally connect with emotional assistance.

- Physical Support

These are actual, palpable kinds of support. In order for you to gain, someone in your network must give up a resource.

- Informational Support

These are recommendations, data, counsel, or other insights to help you. Depending on the sort of information, this might be either personal or professional.

- Appraisal Support

Though they don't center on information directly related to self-evaluation, they are comparable to informational situations. Under this area is constructive criticism.

Deciding Who Should Offer Each Kind of Support

These are all valid and helpful types of support in different contexts. It's also critical to realize that many times, they will come from wildly disparate members of your support system.

For instance, it would be quite OK for your partner to love and support you when you're going through tough times trying to achieve your goals in order to offer emotional support. As your life partner, they can offer an exclusive perspective that others in your network might not have. Parents or close friends who know you better and have more personal connection to you can also provide emotional support.

In contrast, a professional mentor is more likely to give you informational support by expanding your knowledge and providing you with the viewpoint of someone who has probably already achieved what you are trying to accomplish.

A competent manager or supervisor can give you regular appraisal support by offering insightful criticism or comments that can improve your performance and maximize your efforts as you pursue your objectives.

A close friend or mentor might be prepared to lend you initial capital for your firm, or your spouse might be open to working longer hours so you can dedicate more time to growing it. These are just a few examples of the many people who might provide physical assistance.

All forms of social support are equally vital and effective, regardless of their specific form. The more difficult the task at hand appears, the larger your support system will probably need to be. As your objectives broaden, you'll discover that every kind of assistance is perfectly matched to a specific facet of completing that work.

Returning to our previous example of qualifying for the CrossFit Games, you would require assistance at every stage of the procedure. Your friends and family will be more understanding if you provide them with emotional support since they would understand how much time you spend at the gym, how rigorous you are about your food, and that you would probably miss a lot of social activities.

Sponsors or gym members that assist in providing money and resources for you to travel to tournaments may be considered instrumental or physical supporters.

Your coach, who customizes your training to best suit your needs, or another athlete you know who has qualified before and is familiar with the requirements would be good sources of informational support.

When it comes to reaching this specific objective, appraisal support might be the most helpful; this includes the buddy or peer who gives you confidence when you enter the competition and persuades you that you are well-prepared. Every step along the path is essential and valuable.

How to Create a Network of Support

Telling people close to you that you are starting a new project or aiming for a new objective can go a long way toward building your support system. Sharing your objectives with your network is a necessary component of creating effective goals.

Friends and relatives will probably be more ready and willing to help when and if they can. That is if they are aware of what you are attempting to achieve. Not only does this foster support, but it also fosters accountability! If you don't want to disappoint those around you and you have the extra help you need when things get very hard, you have a better chance of succeeding.

You should seek elsewhere if the people in your life don't support you or don't understand what you're trying to accomplish. Look for people who share your thoughts or perspective.

Social media has given rise to several Facebook support groups where individuals exchange ideas and opinions. Any major city or region in the globe can have a variety of groups and support networks found with a short Google search. Spend more time with such individuals and start looking for others who share your goals and aspirations.

Your genes are expressed differently depending on the environment you spend time in, which ultimately shapes who you become. You are the average of the five people you spend the most time with.

It is important to surround yourself with like-minded people so that you can join other people's networks and expand your own network of support. A wonderful place to start is with the people in your gym! Seek out people with comparable objectives in your classes or events, and cooperate to make each other successful.

Motivate individuals in your vicinity to strive harder and establish more ambitious objectives. Always aim to underpromise and overdeliver; make an extra effort to help people and observe how that support comes back to you.

Another excellent resource are mentors. These are people who have attained a degree of accomplishment in their industry that you eventually hope to reach. Relationships between mentors and mentees are quite beneficial because they may educate you on how to avoid the mistakes that they unavoidably made along the way.

The best teacher in life is failure, but you can save a lot of time and frustration by learning from others who have been there before how to avoid common traps. Almost invariably, mentors like their role as mentors! If you believe someone can help and guide you, don't be afraid to reach out to them; chances are they will seize the chance.

When should I switch up my support system?

It's crucial to recognize when your support system is no longer working for you, as you really are the sum of the people you surround yourself with. Setting lofty objectives can occasionally make people around you uncomfortable due to your tenacity and resolve.

Some individuals in life are quite happy to stay average, and when you strive toward something new, they frequently try to put out the flame in your eyes first. If negativity seems to be all around you and you're not getting the help you need, think about shifting who you turn to for assistance.

The relationships in your support system should be mutually beneficial; you should receive the same level of value from them. You should think about removing people from your life or spending less time with them if you discover that they are taking much more from you than they are giving. As harsh as it may sound, you simply cannot afford to allow other people to sap your motivation and keep you from reaching your objectives.

On the other hand, your support system needs to adapt as your goals do. Your network will always include your friends and family if you have them. But, you might have to adjust your network if your objectives change in order to get the assistance and support you require. The peers and mentors needed to develop a successful business are probably very different from those needed to qualify for the CrossFit Games.

Make sure people in your support system are truly assisting you in reaching your objectives by conducting regular audits of them. Recognize that your support system will probably vary slightly depending on your objectives as well!

Make an Investment in Yourself

Most jobs are nearly impossible to finish if you approach them alone. Recognize that your support system frequently has to change as well, especially when you achieve your goals and they combine to create larger, more ambitious objectives.

Look for mentors who have already traveled that path and try to pick up as much knowledge as you can from individuals who have insightful things to share. The best investment you can make is in yourself, so surround yourself with positive people who can help you learn important things and try to take in as much of that knowledge as you can. Rely on your network of support when obstacles arise, as they certainly will, to help you stay afloat and eventually succeed.

Additionally, you must be prepared to offer the assistance and direction that people in your immediate vicinity may occasionally require. Developing a support system is a two-way street where you have to give as much as you receive. Your support system will be one of your most important tools for achieving your objectives, no matter what shape it takes!

CHAPTER 13

The Roots And Remedies

What Sets Off Triggers for Habits?

Because habit cues affect the intricacies of habits, it is useful to know what generates them. The following are some crucial regions where habit triggers emerge:

- **Emotions:**

One of the hardest environments for the establishment of habits is the emotional realm. Emotional cues might cause people to overeat even when they are not hungry. Anxious people are prone to a variety of emotional cues that could overwhelm them.

- **People:**

Habits are formed in part by the behavior of other people. A lot of stress has been brought on by social media's growth of emotions of inadequacy, loneliness, and dissatisfaction.

- **Time:**

A lot of habit structures are produced by time. It is an essential cue for many different types of behaviors in social, professional, and domestic contexts. The formation of isolation-centric practices is influenced by time.

- **Place:**

People are sensitive to clues from their surroundings. If you have experienced trauma, you may get a panic attack just by going back to the scene or to a setting that is comparable.

Major causes of the habit loop includes:

1. Environmental Cues:

Our surroundings are rich with stimuli that can trigger habitual responses. These cues can be anything from the sight of a familiar object to the sound of a particular song. For example, walking into a coffee shop and smelling the aroma of freshly brewed coffee can trigger the habit of ordering a cup, even if we hadn't planned on it. Our brains usually relate certain environmental cues with some particular behaviors, making them strong triggers for habits.

2. Time of Day:
Our supposed internal body clock, which we call the circadian rhythm, helps greatly in regulating our daily activities. Certain habits become tied to specific times of the day due to this natural rhythm. For example, waking up at the same time each morning can trigger the habit of going for a run or making breakfast. Similarly, feeling hungry around meal times prompts us to eat, reinforcing the habit of regular meals.

3. Emotional States:
Our emotions can serve as potent triggers for habits, both positive and negative. When we experience stress, boredom, or anxiety, our brains seek out familiar behaviors that provide comfort or distraction. Stress-eating, nail-biting, and grabbing our phones to check social media can all result from this. As coping strategies for particular emotional states, these actions get profoundly embedded over time.

4. Social Cues:
Human behavior is highly influenced by the actions of others and social norms. Observing the behaviors of

Beyond Regular Habits

those around us or finding ourselves in social situations can trigger habits without us even realizing it. For example, seeing friends or family members reach for snacks during a movie night may prompt us to do the same, even if we're not hungry. Social cues play a major role in helping to shape our habits and behaviors.

5. Visual Cues:
Our brains are highly responsive to visual stimuli, and certain images or symbols can act as triggers for habits. The advertising and branding sectors of business make use of this method by relating products with their specific visual cues that would prompt consumer reactions. For example, seeing a familiar brand logo or advertisement can trigger the habit of purchasing a particular product, even if we hadn't planned on it.

6. Habitual Actions:
Engaging in one habit can often trigger another, creating a chain reaction of behaviors. For example, finishing dinner may trigger the habit of cleaning up the kitchen, followed by the habit of winding down for bed. These regular action sequences get entwined, one flowing naturally into the next, forming our everyday rituals and routines.

7. Location or Setting:

Certain places or environments can serve as powerful cues for habits. Our brains rapidly make the connection between particular places and specific actions, therefore making them reflexive reactions to our environment. For example, walking into a gym may trigger the habit of exercising, while entering a kitchen may prompt the habit of cooking or snacking. These environmental clues are quite important in forming our routines and actions.

8. Preceding Actions:

The actions immediately preceding a habit can serve as cues that trigger the behavior. For example, turning off the TV at night may trigger the habit of getting ready for bed, including brushing teeth and changing into pajamas. Our brains automatically respond to particular conditions or occurrences by associating subsequent actions.

9. Physiological States:

Our bodies send signals when we have specific physiological needs, such as hunger, thirst, or fatigue. These bodily sensations can act as powerful triggers for habits that satisfy these needs. For example, feeling thirsty may trigger the habit of reaching for a glass of water, while feeling tired may prompt the habit of taking a nap or reaching for caffeine. Our brains quickly learn to recognize these physiological cues and respond with appropriate behaviors.

10. Thought Patterns:
Our thoughts and mental associations can also act as triggers for habits. When we dwell on a particular problem or worry, our brains may automatically seek out familiar behaviors that provide relief or distraction.

For example, feeling anxious may trigger the habit of seeking reassurance from a friend or loved one, while feeling overwhelmed may prompt the habit of making a to-do list to regain a sense of control. These thought patterns can become deeply ingrained as habitual responses to specific mental states or situations.

Properly understanding all these triggers is important to learn about our routines and actions. When we take note of the cues that prompt our actions, we can begin to control our habits and make intentional choices that are in line with our goals and values.

Breaking the Cycle
If unbridled, habits can drive us down pathways of self-destruction and stagnation even if they can be extremely effective instruments for productivity and efficiency. Understanding how the habit cycle works and

picking up techniques for escaping bad patterns and developing good ones are therefore crucial. Let us now analyze practical tactics and ways for ending the loop of bad habits, reprogramming our behavior, and creating positive changes that we desire.

How to get out of the loop

Since the process of breaking a habit is typically more involved than just stopping the behavior, habits are frequently hard to break. Even while you might really want to quit checking your phone during work breaks, you generally won't see any significant progress unless you break through the habit loop as a whole.

Though it takes a few steps, change is achievable. A proven way to get out of the habit loop includes the following steps:

- Determine the routine first

Since the routine usually only relates to the habit you wish to eliminate, figuring it out is the easy part. That habit may be the reason you're "sleeping in until you're dangerously close to running late for work". In order to get a few more minutes of sleep, your routine may then include rolling over and turning off the alarm.

- Experiment with other incentives

Generally, habits form when certain behaviors result in rewards. In addition to entertainment, your phone can deliver positive news and messages from loved ones. It becomes second nature to continually pick up your phone in order to get these benefits.

Not only can sleeping in keep you warmer in bed than waking up to a chilly, dark morning, but it may also help you feel more rested. You can also postpone your morning routine for an additional few minutes when you oversleep. You can experiment with rewards that provide comparable fulfillment by examining the benefits of a certain routine for yourself.

A few days spent making little changes to your routine can provide some clarity on the specific benefits you receive. Record your feelings as you test out each new reward. Perhaps one day you will choose to try an entertainment reward like reading for ten minutes instead of going for your phone. One more time, you attempt diversion by brewing a cup of tea.

After the event, note a few thoughts or feelings right away, and again after 15 minutes. Did the two new activities satisfy the same desire? Or do you still get the compulsion to pick up your phone?

- Investigate your triggers

Breaking a habit starts with figuring out the precise indicators that set off your pattern. Do you recall the four categories of cues? Here they are once more: Location, time, emotional state, and last action of those nearby.

Take note of those potential indications each time you find yourself going through the same motions. You can detect the possible triggers more clearly and spot any patterns if you write them down. After a few days of trying this, review your notes to see if anything jumps out. Perhaps a particular friend group or time of day sets off the habit.

- Figure out how to avoid those cues

You can create a special strategy to stop your habit loop from repeating itself by identifying the three components of it. Consider the practice of sleeping in:

Your bed served as your cue, as did your alarm clock set for six a.m. Since getting to bed earlier didn't make it any easier to get up, you weren't yearning for more sleep. It was also not the chilly morning you had been fearing. You were still unable to get out of bed even with a warm robe kept beneath your pillow to put on first thing in the morning.

You eventually come to the realization that your prize is the postponement of your daily routine: you choose to remain in bed rather than take on the task of brewing coffee and getting ready for the day. You can create a strategy by recognizing your habit loop and making the necessary preparations the night before, such as purchasing a programmable coffee pot. When you get out of bed on time, your reward is freshly brewed coffee waiting for you.

Beyond Regular Habits

CONCLUSION

Success Stories

Oprah Winfrey is among the most well-known and prosperous individuals on the planet. Her journey from modest beginnings to becoming one of the most powerful philanthropists, business women, and media moguls inspires many. We will look at Oprah's hardships, her early career in the media, her charitable endeavors, her business endeavors, and the lessons we may take from her.

Oprah Winfrey: Who is she?

American media executive, actress, talk show host, philanthropist, and businesswoman Oprah Winfrey is well-known. What made her most well-known was her talk show, the Oprah Winfrey Show, which she hosted from 1986 until 2011.

Oprah is considered the richest African American of the 20th century and is among the most successful individuals on the planet. She is listed as one of the most significant people in the world by Time magazine as well. Oprah inspires and motivates a lot of people, and her journey from hardship to success inspires many more. She is the ideal illustration of how tenacity and diligence can produce incredible results.

Early Challenges

Oprah was born in Mississippi in 1954 to a teenage mother who was on her own. As a child, she was subjected to cruelty and misery. She was transferred to live with her father when she was nine, and he gave her a rigorous and orderly upbringing. Oprah was a gifted student who was admitted to a prominent school in spite of her difficulties.

Oprah was raped and mistreated by family members and other community members when she was fourteen years old. Oprah persevered in keeping her academic concentration despite these upsetting experiences. With a full scholarship, she attended Tennessee State University to study communication.

Career Start-Up

Oprah started her career as a news anchor in Baltimore after graduating from college. She became well-known very fast for her fervent and knowledgeable reporting. Her television program, The Oprah Winfrey Show, which went on to become one of the most popular talk shows in history, was offered to her in 1984.

For 25 years, the Oprah Winfrey Show was the highest-rated talk show in the country. Oprah conducted interviews with prominent global public leaders, politicians, and celebrities on her show. She also spoke about significant subjects including violence, poverty, and prejudice.

How she Became a Media Mogul

Oprah established Harpo Productions, her production firm, in the late 1990s. Oprah produced her movies, TV series, and books via Harpo. One of the most successful magazines in the world, O, The Oprah Magazine, was also started by her.

Oprah began her radio program, Oprah Radio, and her television network, OWN: The Oprah Winfrey Network, in addition to her television shows. Oprah has become one of the most powerful media moguls in the world, reaching millions of people worldwide through these platforms.

Oprah's Generosity

Oprah has benefited others by using her success. The Oprah Winfrey Foundation, which she founded, provides funding for humanitarian causes all over the world. Through her foundation, Oprah has given millions of dollars to organizations in the fields of education, the environment, health, and social justice.

Oprah also founded the Oprah Winfrey Leadership Academy for Girls in South Africa, which offers resources and instruction to adolescent females. In South Africa, the academy is recognized for having positively impacted the lives of hundreds of young women.

Oprah's Commercial Activities

Oprah has used her success to launch successful enterprises. In 2009, she launched The Oprah Magazine Collection, her clothing line. The collection was a big hit, selling out at retailers all around the world.

Oprah also unveiled O, The Oprah Magazine Skincare, her skincare collection. The brand was well received for employing natural ingredients and was a big success.

Oprah has also published her own book and turned into a venture investor, funding a number of prosperous firms.

Oprah's Motivational Sayings

Oprah is well-known for her wisecracks and motivational sayings. These are a few of her most motivational sayings:

- "To live the life of your dreams is the biggest adventure you can embark on."
- "There is more in life to celebrate the more you honor and celebrate your life."
- "Gratitude for what you already have will bring you more. You will never, ever have enough if you focus on what you lack."
- "You will have to be grateful for more the more you are grateful for what you have."
- "The most important thing I've learnt is to always stay loyal to who you are."
- "The secret to fulfilling a dream is to put significance above success; only then will even the little victories and steps you take along the way have more significance."
- "Your relationship with yourself is the most significant one you will ever have."
- "It is your responsibility to control the energy you bring into this room."

Life Lessons From Oprah

Oprah Winfrey's inspirational tale shows how perseverance and hard effort can lead to amazing things. The following are some things we can take away from Oprah:

1. Have faith in yourself: Oprah overcame adversity and hardship by having faith in herself, which helped her succeed.
2. Take chances: Oprah achieved her success because she took chances and went after her dreams.
3. Don't be scared to fail: Despite Oprah's repeated failures, she never let it deter her from achieving her objectives.
4. Give back: Oprah has contributed millions of dollars to philanthropic causes by using her fortune to assist others.
5. Remain focused: In spite of her challenges, Oprah never wavered from her objectives.

In summary,

Oprah Winfrey's path is a monument to tenacity, drive, and foresight. Her success story showcases her abilities as an entrepreneur and includes not only how she rose to the highest level of media celebrity but also her incredible venture into the business sector.

This entrepreneur's tale addresses the question of how Oprah Winfrey launched her company with passion, ingenuity, and a keen grasp of her target market. It also offers priceless lessons about beginning from scratch.

Beyond her business endeavors and the astounding wealth they have brought her, however, the real question is: How is Oprah Winfrey an exceptional entrepreneur? Her success is based on making a lasting impression rather than merely monetary rewards.

Oprah Winfrey was driven not only by her own accomplishments but also by her desire to encourage, empower, and uplift others. She embodies the reasons that countless businesspeople throughout the world find her encouraging. Let her tale serve as a source of inspiration and direction for you as you embark on your own journey.

Beyond Regular Habits

Beyond Regular Habits

www.ingramcontent.com/pod-product-compliance
Lightning Source LLC
Chambersburg PA
CBHW071921210526
45479CB00002B/505